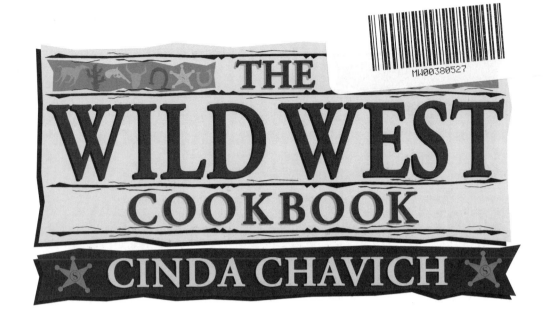

THE WILD WEST COOKBOOK

CINDA CHAVICH

Robert
ROSE

The Wild West Cookbook

For complete cataloguing data, see page 4.

DESIGN AND PAGE COMPOSITION:	MATTHEWS COMMUNICATIONS DESIGN
PHOTOGRAPHY:	MARK T. SHAPIRO
ART DIRECTION, FOOD PHOTOGRAPHY:	SHARON MATTHEWS
FOOD STYLIST:	KATE BUSH
PROP STYLIST:	CHARLENE ERRICSON
MANAGING EDITOR:	PETER MATTHEWS
RECIPE EDITORS/TEST KITCHEN:	LESLEIGH LANDRY, JAN MAIN
INDEXER:	BARBARA SCHON
COLOR SCANS & FILM:	POINTONE GRAPHICS

Cover photo: PORK AND BEEF CHILI WITH ANCHO SAUCE (PAGE 117)

Distributed in the U.S. by:
Firefly Books (U.S.) Inc.
P.O. Box 1338
Ellicott Station
Buffalo, NY   14205

Distributed in Canada by:
Stoddart Publishing Co. Ltd.
34 Lesmill Road
North York, Ontario
M3B 2T6

ORDER LINES
Tel: (416) 499-8412
Fax: (416) 499-8313

ORDER LINES
Tel: (416) 445-3333
Fax: (416) 445-5967

Published by: Robert Rose Inc. • 156 Duncan Mill Road, Suite 12
Toronto, Ontario, Canada M3B 2N2   Tel: (416) 449-3535

Printed in Canada

12345678 BP 01 00 99 98

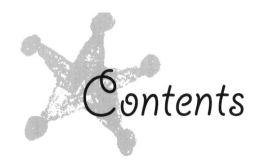

Contents

Canadian Cataloguing in Publication Data

Chavich, Cinda
    The wild west cookbook

Includes index.

ISBN 1-896503-65-9

1. Cookery, American – Western. 2. Cookery, Canadian – Prairie style
I. Title.

TX715.2.W47C42 1998   641.5978   C98-931350-6

This book is dedicated to my husband, Delbert, and to all of those people who have shared their recipes, their love of food and their inspiration with me over the years. But especially to two women who were both warm, welcoming cooks and whom I shall miss — my grandmother, Danita Chavich, and my friend and colleague, Cynny Willet.

Cowboy Cooking and the Wild West

Travel is what defines the cowboy of both yesterday and today.

High plains drifters, itinerant ranch workers, or modern rodeo riders — cowboys have always embodied the ideal of the rootless wanderer, just as likely to blow into town on a dusty chinook wind or drift right on out again.

Like the plains buffalo, the rattlesnake or the crafty coyote, the range of the cowboy is wide — a strip of North American desert, prairie and rocky mountain wilderness that stretches from the Gulf states of southern Texas and New Mexico, clear up to the cool Canadian Rockies. Whether you hail from Tulsa, Oklahoma or Three Hills, Alberta — Albuquerque or Amarillo — the cowboy is a part of local history, folklore and everyday life.

And no matter where you call home, there's probably a few cowboy memories in your past, too — whether it was playing stagecoach with cap guns on the back steps, riding real horses on the farm during summer vacations, or simply settling down on Sunday night in front of a fuzzy black-and-white TV for another installment of *Bonanza*.

The cowboy life is a romantic one for most, firmly settled in our modern nostalgia for simpler times. Life would be so much easier if you could just ride off into the sunset or, like Gene Autry, break the tension with a soothing ballad.

But for the last 150 years, the reality of cowboy life has been lived by many Westerners in both Canada and the U.S. — a tableau of natural beauty and big skies, dotted with the realities of drought, isolation, low grain and cattle prices, and other prairie hardships.

Because it was first to be settled, America's Old West was also first to see the cowboy. These early American ranch workers learned their cowpunching skills from Mexican *vaqueros*, borrowing their practical style of clothing — including wide-brimmed hats and protective leather chaps — and learning the riding and roping skills needed to herd cattle and horses on the open range.

Like the tumbling tumbleweeds, the range of cowboys drifting throughout the West, expanded with the cattle business. Trailing cattle from the Texas plains to the railheads of Kansas for sale to slaughterhouses in Chicago was all part of the cowboy's job. Some early Texans drove cattle from the Midwest, all the way to New York City. By the early 1880s, they were driving Texas longhorns as far north as Canada, beginning the north-south cowboy migration that is still as common as the western bluebird or Canada goose.

The cowboy was a part-time worker, usually a seasonal hand who moved from one outfit to the next as work was available. Those who traveled from Texas, Wyoming and New Mexico brought their customs and cuisines with them. Even today, it's as common to see a Texas chili on the menu in Calgary (where it's rarely hot enough to grow such a spicy pepper) as it is to eat prairie bison in the Colorado Rockies.

With all of our shared history, geography and climate, this is no surprise. Anyone familiar with the regional political debates in both Canada and the U.S., knows we have more in common with our north-south neighbors across the border than some of our own citizens from eastern or western coastal regions — mainly a function of climate and indigenous flora, fauna and food.

So it also comes as no surprise that many cowboy customs are interchangeable, wherever cowboys work and live throughout the West. Whether it's the myth of the tall, silent gunslinger or the cowboy creed of loyalty above all to his outfit, things are the same among this breed throughout the West.

Let's look at this reality as it relates to food.

Beef still reigns on the range from Alberta to Abilene, and you'll find the best beef steaks, roasts and ribs in the world on any cowboy menu. Cowboys all eat flapjacks and biscuits, strong coffee, stews and chili — holdovers from the days when chuckwagon cooks fed them these basics on the range. And there's still a strong reliance on root vegetables and other storage crops in western cooking, as well as wild foods like game and berries, and old-fashioned prairie cooking that came with early waves of settlers from European countries like Britain, Scotland, Ireland, Germany, Italy, France and Eastern Europe.

From the cowboy roots in Mexico came the flavors of searing chilies, corn and chocolate — and today nachos, tamale pies and tortillas are solidly enshrined in western menus.

But back a hundred years ago, when cowboys were roving the range, ranch hands had their dinner-on-the-hoof and they took whatever Cookie (a common handle for a chuckwagon cook) was dishing out.

As one old ranch cook used to say, "you become a great cook when you like to eat."

But all chuckwagon cooks were not created equal, and the best cowboys drifted to those outfits where the man behind the grub liked to eat and learned to cook. That was the only perk a cowboy could expect from his employer — and good cooks were hard to find.

With basic staples like flour, bacon, beans, lard, cornmeal and sugar, they offered some good chuck from the back of their wagons, based on the meat at hand, mostly wild game and beef. From biscuits and jerky to baked beans, prairie oysters and flapjacks, no man in the saddle ever starved.

Back at the ranch, farm wives and ranch cooks tended gardens, raised chickens and pigs and baked wild fruit or rhubarb pies in big, blackened wood stoves. In the southern climes of Texas and New Mexico, the meals may have been spiced with chilies and served with tortillas, but basic meat-and-potatoes fare was (and is) the mainstay of all cowboy cooks.

Some cooks rode the range with the cowboys during long treks and drives to market. But day-to-day chuckwagons often returned to the ranch after dinner on the range. The practice of tossing the hot stove in the back of the wagon and racing back to the ranch became an event at rodeos — and now pro rodeo cowboys vie for a $100,000 prize every year during the chuckwagon races at the Calgary Stampede.

Today things are different on the range.

Cowboys carry cell phones and watch the markets via computers in their hefty pick-up trucks. Some still rely on their own "cookie" to feed them chuckwagon-style during annual round-ups in the foothills, but you'll see cowboys in the city, too, snacking on spicy Thai chicken wings or eating Italian.

While today's cowboy country cuisine is a melting pot of all world cuisines, the early influences came from the first settlers.

In Canada, the English and French were the first to venture out West, but they were soon followed by Swiss mountain guides, Italian and Chinese railway workers, Germans and Eastern Europeans. In the U.S., similar waves of European immigrants made their way by wagon train to settle the western wilderness. In southern states like Texas, there was a distinct Spanish influence and up to one-third of working cowboys were either Mexican- or African-Americans.

All brought their own cooking traditions, but were forced to adapt their daily meals to the harsh conditions and meager supplies at hand. They learned from the local native tribes about foraging for edible roots and berries, and added all manner of local game to their menus.

The Native people lived off the land — Plains Indians like Cree, Crow, Blackfoot, Apache and Cheyenne relied on wild meat and fowl for their diet, which consisted mainly of dried buffalo meat, pemmican, game (moose and elk) and fish. They augmented this with berries, Vitamin-C-rich rose hips, wild onions and parsnips, and mint from the mountains for tea. These were nomadic tribes, moving around the prairie from summer to winter camps to hunt buffalo. Further south, Navajo, Hopi and Zuni Indians made permanent homes in Arizona, southern Utah and New Mexico, carving elaborate villages out of the sandstone cliffs and planting crops like corn, beans and squash, also adding buffalo, game and wild plants like cactus to their diets. These southern tribes even raised sheep and domestic turkey, and the flavors spread northward with the trading between settled and nomadic tribes throughout the West.

The first immigrants to North America arrived from Europe three centuries ago, mainly settling in eastern areas. It wasn't until after 1840 that the bulk of the 300,000 pioneers made the trek out West along the Oregon trail. By 1860, the white population had grown from 20,000 to nearly 1 million, with many of these settlers staking claims and displacing the free-roaming natives from their homelands.

By 1865, there were stagecoach lines as far west as Denver, Santa Fe and Salt Lake City. In Canada, farmers were heading out in Red River carts, dragging their family possessions to prairie farmsteads past the end of the rail line in Winnipeg. (By 1885, that railway spanned Canada from sea to sea; the transcontinental U.S. railway was finished in 1869.)

The wave of settlement continued as pioneers traveled by train and covered wagon on trails to Santa Fe and California via bustling towns in Missouri. On the trails they carried the staples of the chuckwagon cook, augmented by wild foods and sourdough breads baked on the campfire. When they arrived in western settlements, they planted what food they could grow in the area, raised poultry and pigs, and collected native foods from fields and forests.

In 1891, half of Alberta's population was Native, but by 1930 an eclectic mix of immigrants had arrived — mainly British, German, Ukrainian, French, Scandinavian, Dutch and Polish. Chinese workers had come to build the railways and many ended up as ranch cooks or restaurant owners in small prairie towns. A similar demographic had settled the American plains a generation earlier, influenced by earlier Hispanic settlers.

Many early immigrants to the Canadian West were also Americans, mainly the cattle men and cowboys who arrived with their herds, bringing their southern cowboy culture of foods like corn and spicy chilies.

Early settlers brought their European farming techniques and livestock to the prairies, developing a cuisine that mixed ethnic heritage with Native traditions and availability, enjoying everything from wild duck, game and bannock to dandelion greens and spruce beer.

Since then, new waves of immigrants have brought many new ethnic influences to the kitchens of the western heartland of North America. From its Anglo-French and European roots, prairie cooking has evolved to embrace the traditions of East Indians, Thais and Malays from the East; Caribbean and Central Americans from the South; and native Canadians right here at home. In the American West, much of this diversity has been lost to that country's melting pot ideal of assimilation, but in Canada, where a multicultural mosaic is encouraged, many of these unique cuisines have been planted and have flourished.

Today we're also learning a new appreciation of the cowboy culture that opened the West. We're searching the old recipe books and resurrecting a regional cuisine for this century — inspired by the cowboy cooking on the range, but updated for health and modern cooking methods.

We no longer have to bake our bread and make our beef stews in cast iron Dutch ovens surrounded by campfire coals, but we yearn for those simple flavors that hark back to our western cooking roots.

This collection of recipes includes both the old-fashioned rhubarb pies of grandma's kitchen, and the bean salsas we now love to snack on around the campfire or on the deck.

The cuisine of the cowboy has changed with the times, but just enough to keep it current. We still love our beef and beans. We still organize international chili cook-offs, pride ourselves for our pancakes and make some of the country's best beer from our own fields of golden barley. Slow Texas-style barbecue is a staple at rodeos from San Antonio, Texas to Saskatchewan.

From Native foods like wild mint, mountain mushrooms and Saskatoon berries to the game of the forests and trout of the streams, western cuisine has indigenous inspirations. Add to that the farm-based economy of grains like wheat, corn and barley; the ranch tradition of raising beef cattle, chickens, pork and lamb, and new livestock like buffalo, farmed elk and ostrich; and the market gardening belts where vegetables flourish, and there's plenty of raw material for a creative cuisine.

Today's cowboy cuisine is still hearty, homey and uncomplicated — but there is also a new refinement. Harvests of trendy blue potatoes and designer beans are the new raw materials. Creative sausage makers have risen above the everyday pork sausage popular at pancake break-fasts to make apple chicken sausages and spicy Italian versions that end up in searing chilies and stews. Today's butchers — like those at Valbella Meats in Canmore, Alberta — are turning local game into our own indigenous gourmet foods, from air-dried buffalo prosciutto to peppered dusk breast, elk smokies and wild boar pâté.

The same thing is happening in the American south. Pendery's, spice merchants in Fort Worth since 1870, is now doing a roaring mail-order business in the kind of flavors that put the Lone Star state on the map — especial-ly various peppers and chili blends such as Chiltomaline, DeWitt Clinton Pendery's 1890 mixture of ground Texas chili pods, cumin, oregano and other spices, perhaps the West's first chili powder. But even Pendery's has found fusion flavors deep in the heart of Texas, and now their range of herbs and spices ranges from bright yellow anchiote seed to ground cardamom, ginseng and crystallized ginger; the catalogue also offers Indian masalas and Moroccan *charmoula* seasonings.

Cowboy cooking has become more interesting and unusual, but it's familiar all the same. You won't find any tropical fruits or Asian spices in this cowboy cuisine — but maybe there's something just as interesting from the forest or farm you haven't seen on your plate before.

The old staples like cornmeal and beans that cowboy Cookie worked with on the range are all here. You'll find recipes for the the roundup beef stews and chilies, the old-fashioned bread and pies, and the crispy prairie oysters cooked up in a blackened skillet at branding time.

No *mahi-mahi* on the menu — but lots of beef, lamb and pork, free-range poultry and buffalo. There are rib-sticking chilies and beans, delicate dishes made with local trout, and stylish flans filled with native Saskatoon berries.

It's a celebration of food from the Wild West, a new way of looking at the cuisine of the cowboy.

So travel back in time and try some comfort-able chuck and some newfangled western food — hearty, healthy and homemade.

Come and get it!

The Wild West Pantry

Beans. A long-time staple in the cowboy cook's larder, beans are great in soups or spiced up with chilies, onions and garlic. Or try them puréed as low-fat dips, mixed with ground meat in burgers or in old-fashioned bean salads.
To prepare dry beans for cooking: Pick over beans for dirt and rocks that sometimes make their way into the mix. Soak overnight or use the following 1-hour quick-soak method:
In a pot, cover beans with water and bring to a boil. Cook 2 minutes; cover and remove from heat. Let beans soak for 1 hour; drain.
Don't salt your beans before cooking or they'll never soften. Beans can take 1 to 2 hours to cook, depending on their age and original con-dition. Don't mix beans before cooking as dif-ferent beans never cook at the same rate.
When cooked, 1 lb (500 g) dried beans equals 6 or 7 cups (1.5 to 1.75 L) cooked beans. You can freeze presoaked and/or cooked beans for convenience and taste — they're better than canned beans.

Although their texture is inferior for dishes using whole beans, canned beans are simple and fast to use, especially for dips or refried bean dishes. Rinse and drain canned beans before adding to soups and stews.
Lentils and split peas need no soaking and cook in 20 minutes to 1 hour, depending on the variety.

Beef. Always look for AAA Canadian beef or U.S. Prime beef; this has the highest fat mar-belling and is best for grilling and roasting. Lower grades and less tender cuts should be braised or stewed — in fact, you sacrifice flavor if you use a prime cut in the stew or soup pot. Roasting beef is also popular. Hip cuts (such as round, rump and sirloin tip roasts) are best when started in a very hot (500 °F [260 °C]) oven for 30 minutes, uncovered, then cooked to desired doneness at a reduced temperature of 275° F (140° C). Adding 1 cup (250 mL) water to the roast pan after the initial high-tempera-ture searing helps keep the roast moist and juicy.

Beer. The trend toward microbrewing began in the western U.S. cities of San Francisco and Seattle and has spread like a prairie fire throughout the West. Of course, beer is still the beverage of choice in this part of the world and all of the major players — from Coors to Molson's — make their beer here. Microwbrewers have had a huge impact on the quality of beer being consumed today. When Ed McNally started brewing Big Rock beer in Calgary a short decade ago, strong ales were almost unheard of. Now they're pulled from taps in specialty pubs from Swift Current to San Francisco and Big Rock has grown into one of the country's most successful micro-breweries, recently expanding to a size so large it's now dubbed a regional brewery.

Berries. In the summer months, wild or U-pick berries can be found everywhere in the West. Among them, Saskatoon berries are the quintessential prairie berry. Also known as the service-berry, these bush-grown berries resemble a blueberry but with a distinctive sweet flavor and drier texture. The wild variety can still be found growing in the coulees and along river banks across the western prairies, but you can also plant your own domestic Saskatoon berry bushes and harvest crops in your own backyard. Other berries, from wild strawberries and raspberries to low-bush and high-bush cranberries, chokecherries, Nanking cherries and wild currants have been used by natives, settlers and current prairie residents for hundreds of years.

Buffalo. Buffalo or bison (their proper name) once roamed the prairies in massive herds, ranging from New York to the Rocky Mountains and from Mexico to the Northwest Territories. Brought back from near extinction in the 19th century, buffalo or bison meat has gained popularity on the prairies in recent years. While still expensive to buy, it is being raised on about 200 Alberta ranches today. Bison are grass-fed (unlike cattle, which are grain-fed) and naturally raised with no growth hormones; so buffalo meat is considered particularly clean and healthy. Buffalo is lean and flavorful, with a taste very similar to beef. Because of its low fat content (2.4 grams of fat per 100 grams), it must be cooked at lower temperatures

(275° F [140° C] for roasting) and should always be served medium or medium-rare.

Bulgar or Cracked Wheat. Bulgar is made from whole kernels of wheat which are boiled, then dried and broken into bits. Cracked wheat is a different product; it is simply coarsely ground raw wheat, with the wheat germ removed to improve shelf life. Cracked wheat needs to be cooked, while bulgar only needs soaking to rehydrate.

Canola oil. This light-tasting vegetable oil is produced across the prairies — Canada's own answer to the Mediterranean diet. Like olive oil, touted for it's cholesterol-friendly monounsaturated fats, canola oil is also high in monounsaturates and is recommended when a strong flavor is not desired, as in baking and frying.

Corn. Every summer, Albertans await the sweet corn grown around the town of Taber, near Lethbridge in southern Alberta. At every roadside, you'll see half-ton trucks piled with corn and hand-lettered signs simply announcing Taber Corn. This is when cobs go for a dollar or two a dozen and you can enjoy it simply boiled or grilled in the husk and smothered with melted butter.

Grain. With countless flour mills and cereal producers located throughout the prairies, the West is a primary source for wheat, barley and cereal grains around the world. Barley is another grain grown all over the West. Whether it goes into our great micro-brewed beers or a pot of soup, there are lots of uses for this healthy grain. Pot and pearl barley are both processed — pot barley has the bran and germ removed, while pearl barley is even further processed and cooks faster. Both work well in soups, pilafs and casseroles in place of rice and are a source of cholesterol-lowering soluble fiber.

Jerky. Beef jerky is a cowboy favorite — slices of lean beef that have been marinated and spiced, then dried to chewy perfection for carrying along on the cattle drive or just gnawing on the way home in the truck. While you can make your own jerky, a great, preservative-free local supply can be had from Longview Meats, where Len Kirk turns out those chewy sticks you see shrink wrapped by the till at gas stations and corner stores across Alberta, in flavors from original to cracked pepper and barbecue or teriyaki.

Mushrooms. You'll find plenty of mushrooms — both edible and deadly poisonous — on the western prairies and in the Rocky Mountains. The trick, of course, is to make sure you don't eat anything you're not absolutely sure about. Still, with a good guidebook or a seasoned expert, it's fun to hunt down mushrooms. There are two easily identifiable species: the morel and the puffball. Morels have tall, pointed caps, are dark in color and built like a sponge or honeycomb. They appear in the spring in forests and woodlands. Puffballs, as small as a golf ball or as big as a basketball, are found sitting like stones in grassy fields. Don't pick old puffballs — they break easily and send out a smoke of brown spores when poked. Like all mushrooms, puffballs and morels are best simply sautéed in butter with salt and pepper. Or you can add some cream and sherry and reduce for a creamy mushroom sauce to serve over potatoes or toast.

Mustard. Today almost all of the world's mustard seeds come from Saskatchewan, Manitoba and Alberta — 700,000 acres of mustard are harvested here, where the drought- and cold-tolerant crop thrives. India is the only other country that grows some of its own mustard. All others are importers of Canadian mustard seeds, even the famous mustard-makers of Dijon in France. Making mustard is simple — seeds are ground and mixed with sugar, wine or vinegar, herbs and spices. The more of the seed coat or hull that's left in the mix, the spicier the mustard will be. You can make your own homemade mustard by mixing dry mustard powder and water, wine or fruit juice to form a paste. Let it stand for 30 minutes and season it with any of your favorite herbs, from thyme to tarragon. Sweeten mustard with brown sugar or honey as desired, spike it with scotch or cognac, and add it to sauces, dressings and sandwiches.

Rhubarb. Rhubarb is really a vegetable, but one that grows like a weed in the West — and

it's part of every prairie pie maker's pantry. Laced with enough sugar and other flavors (such as orange peel and strawberries), rhubarb has a wonderful sharp flavor that boosts desserts from crumbles and muffins to tarts, and makes a great base for savory sauces and chutneys. The best rhubarb is young and red — some varieties are sweeter and have more color. This is a plant that thrives in the cool mountainous West, from Calgary to Colorado. In the mountain mining town of Silverton, Colorado, the plant is celebrated at an annual festival, complete with parade and rhubarb cooking competition.

Rose hips. Since the wild rose is the official flower of Alberta, the edible rose hip, the seed pod of the rose, warrants a separate mention. Wild rose bushes grow everywhere from the prairies and parkland to the mountains and foothills, short little bushes covered in pale pink or deep rose single blossoms. Behind every flower, an orange-red hip matures in August or September, a thick-skinned seed pod usually best picked after the first frost.
Rose hips are rich in Vitamin C and presumably the rose hip syrup, jellies and other condiments put up by early prairie dwellers saved them from scurvy and other deficiency diseases.
The hips can be cleaned, halved then boiled for 20 minutes to release their juice. Strain and sweeten to taste, usually equal parts rose hips and sugar. Use rose hip juice for beverages or to make jams and jellies.

Trout. Native to western streams and rivers, wild trout is much sought after by sport fishers and farmed trout is a favorite of chefs.
Wild populations include several species of trout — from lake trout and brown trout to brook trout, as well as rainbow trout (the type most often found in supermarkets). This delicate fish is usually cooked whole or in fillets. It is usually available in small 1- to 2-pound (500 g to 1 kg) sizes, although wild fish can be much larger.
Trout may be lightly floured and seasoned for pan-frying, stuffed and baked or smoked. Cold smoked trout is a particular delicacy, eaten like lox or smoked salmon in appetizers, or puréed for smoked trout pâtés.

To remove the backbone and butterfly a whole trout or prepare it for stuffing: Cut through the rib bones along the backbone and work the backbone free in one piece. Then use a thin-bladed knife to scrape the tiny bones away from the flesh.

To bone a whole, cooked trout, cut along the backbone and lift the fillet away from the bone by the tail. The bones and head can now be easily lifted away from the second fillet.

It's not necessary to scale a trout before cooking. The tiny scales are coated with a thin, gelatinous film which gives fresh fish a smooth texture and sparkle. It also helps flour, seasonings and ground nuts adhere to the skin.

Trout flesh can be white or pink, depending on the fish's diet. A pretty pink flesh indicates the trout were probably feasting on freshwater shrimp.

Whisky. Spelled with an "e" in the U.S. — and, Scottish-style, without, in Canada — whisky in the West is made with everything from rye to corn.

Cowboys and other early Americans were known for the great quantities of whisky they consumed, in western saloons and as an instant anesthetic before impromtu operations in many a cowboy flick. Whisky is still a popular drink in the West — rye and Coke being the prairie classic — and a new generation is redis-covering the wonders of single malt scotch.

Wild flowers and edible greens. Many edible flowers grow wild and may be cultivated in western gardens.

When you're planting your flower garden, make room for spicy nasturtiums, violets or violas, marigolds and roses.

All can be scattered over salads for color and interest. Nasturtiums, both leaves and flowers, add a nice peppery bite. (Of course, never eat flowers from roadsides or those that have been sprayed with chemicals or insecticides.)

Violets and violas, which pop up all over the shady spots in my garden, are pretty in salads or decorating desserts. To make candied violets, make a syrup of 4 parts sugar to 1 part water, bring it to a boil and cool. Dip flowers in cooled syrup and let them dry on a rack.or on paper in a low oven You can store them in a box, separated by layers of waxed paper and use them scattered over cakes and ice cream. Rose petals can be candied in a similar way or you can make rose petal tea by drying rose buds and steeping in boiling water.

Native people enjoyed spring greens, from wild mallow and sorrel to lamb's quarters, cooked or fresh long before wild greens became trendy. It's easy to collect greens in the wild or to grow these "weeds" in the backyard to augment summer salads. Dandelions abound and, as long as they haven't been sprayed with chemicals, can be eaten. The flowers may be battered and deep fried, the young leaves are good in salads, the roots can be dried and ground for a coffee-like beverage and the petals can be made into dandelion wine.

For the latter, you'll need a gallon (4 to 5 L) of petals pulled off the flowers steeped for 10 days in a gallon (4 to 5 L) of boiling water in a large crock. Strain into a preserving kettle. Add the peel of an orange and a lemon, plus the flesh (cut up, without the white pith), 4 lbs (2 kg) of sugar; boil for 20 minutes. Return to the crock, add a tablespoon (15 mL) brewer's yeast and cover for 2 days. Pour into a sealed jug, let rest 2 months, then bottle.

For a non-alcoholic dandelion cordial, eliminate the fermentation stage. Pour boiling water over the petals and let stand overnight. The next day, strain and add the sugar, lemon and orange. Let stand for 3 days and strain before serving.

Wild rice. Grown across western Canada, especially in northern Alberta and Saskatchewan, wild rice is actually the seed or grain of an aquatic prairie grass (genus *zizania/aquetica var.*) and is the only native cereal grain in North America.

It grows in the wilderness of northern Canada, and was once harvested only by natives who pulled the grasses down into their canoes where they shook and collected the dried kernels. Now both native and non-native groups plant and harvest the rice commercially, some in special Hovercrafts built to skim over the water and collect the grain in big scoops. But it's still a rare commodity and therefore expensive, sometimes called the caviar of grains.

Low in fat and high in protein and Vitamin B, wild rice is boiled in 3 to 4 times its volume of water or broth, then drained. When cooked, the hard, dark brown kernels split and curl, with a nutty flavor and chewy texture.

eal cowboys in the Wild West wouldn't have known an hors d'oeuvre from a horse's ... well, you get the drift.  Cowboys got up before dawn, bulked up on massive meat-and-beans breakfasts and never stopped for chow before sundown. ✧ Back at camp they didn't dare sneak a snack until Cookie called "Come an' git it" or "Grub pile, come a-runnin' fellers" and then they filled their plates and demolished the meal in silence, washing it all down with gallons of cowboy coffee, strong and black. ✧ If anything, it was the latter that provided a between-meals snack — in the best camps the coffee was always on the fire, as this bit of Tex Taylor's poetry recalls:

> The coffee pot there by the fire was full
>   of Cookie's brew,
> Hot an' black an' strong enough to float
>   an ole hoss shoe.

But these days, even cowboys like to kick back with a beer and a plate of nachos or a smoky quesadilla before sitting down to supper. So here are some ideas for rib-sticking snacks or something to start a meal Western style.

Appetizers

Smoky Cowboy Quesadillas

The quesadilla, grilled crispy and smoky on the barbecue, is the quintessential Western snack — an idea borrowed from our neighbors south of the border but one that works well in cowboy country.

Try making quesadillas with various fillings: chilies and asiago cheese; chopped cooked chicken with avocado and Cheddar; spicy tomato salsa, sliced black olives and farmer's cheese; refried beans, Monterey Jack cheese, avocado or tomato and cilantro. The best quesadillas have just enough filling and cheese to hold together well without being sloppy.

PREHEAT BARBECUE

8	flour tortillas (plain, whole wheat or jalapeno flavor)	8
1 tbsp	olive oil	15 mL
3/4 cup	SPICY SALSA WITH HOT AND SWEET PEPPERS (See recipe, page 23) *or* store-bought salsa	175 mL
4 oz	shredded smoked turkey *or* ham or chicken	125 g
1 cup	shredded Monterey Jack cheese (or combination of cheeses)	250 mL
1	ripe avocado or summer peach or nectarine, slivered	1
1/4 cup	chopped cilantro	50 mL
	Extra salsa as accompaniment	

1. Brush 4 tortillas with olive oil. Place, oiled side down, on a work surface. Divide 3/4 cup (175 mL) salsa among tortillas, spreading over surface. Sprinkle with turkey, cheese, avocado and cilantro. Top with remaining tortillas, brush tops with olive oil and press together firmly.

2. Using a large spatula to lift filled tortillas, carefully set quesadillas on a hot barbecue grill; cook, turning once, until just browned and melted together, about 5 minutes in total. Press quesadillas lightly with a spatula as they cook, to make sure they hold together. Alternatively, cook quesadillas one at a time in a nonstick skillet over medium-high heat, about 3 minutes per side or until golden.

3. Cut each quesadilla into 6 wedges and serve with extra salsa for dipping.

MAKES 6 1/2 CUPS (1.625 L)

Wild West Bean Caviar with Roasted Tomatoes

Use 3 cans (each 19 oz [540 mL]) black beans or black-eyed peas, rinsed and drained, or cook your own starting with 2 1/2 cups (625 mL) dried.

PREHEAT BROILER OR BARBECUE

3	ripe tomatoes	3
2 tbsp	olive oil	25 mL
1/4 cup	red wine vinegar, plus a pinch of granulated sugar *or* balsamic vinegar	50 mL
1 tbsp	lime juice	15mL
3	cloves garlic, minced	3
1/2 tsp	salt	2 mL
6 cups	cooked black beans or black-eyed peas	1.5 L
1/2 cup	chopped red onions	125 mL
1/2 cup	chopped cilantro	125 mL
1	jalapeno pepper, seeded and minced	1
	Corn chips or pita chips	

1. Under the broiler or on the barbecue, cook tomatoes for 10 minutes, turning occasionally, or until charred on all sides. Cool; peel, seed and core. In a food processor, combine tomato flesh, olive oil, vinegar, lime juice, garlic and salt; process until smooth.

2. In a bowl, stir together roasted tomato sauce, beans, red onion, cilantro and jalapeno peppers. Let stand at room temperature for 30 minutes to allow flavors to develop.

3. Serve with corn chips and pita chips for scooping, or serve as a starter salad or side dish.

Tequila Cheese Ball

This is a spicy twist on the old-fashioned cheese ball, a prairie party staple. Makes one large or several small balls.

Use dried New Mexico chilies if anchos are not available.

8 oz	sharp Cheddar cheese, shredded (about 2 cups [500 mL])	250 g
8 oz	mild Cheddar cheese, shredded (about 2 cups [500 mL])	250 g
8 oz	low-fat cream cheese, cut into pieces, warmed to room temperature	250 g
2/3 cup	finely chopped green onions	150 mL
3	cloves garlic, minced	3
2 tbsp	grated orange zest	25 mL
2 tbsp	gold tequila	25 mL
2 tbsp	orange-flavored liqueur	25 mL
2 tsp	curry powder	10 mL
2 tsp	dry mustard	10 mL
1 tsp	ground coriander	5 mL
1/4 tsp	cayenne pepper	1 mL
2	dried ancho chilies, seeded; ground or crushed	2
	Crackers as accompaniment	

1. In a food processor, combine shredded Cheddar, cream cheese, green onions, garlic, orange zest, tequila, orange-flavored liqueur, curry powder, mustard, coriander and cayenne pepper; process until well-mixed, scraping down sides of the bowl as necessary. Transfer to a bowl. Chill until slightly firm.

2. Turn mixture onto a piece of plastic wrap; form into a large ball. Alternatively, divide mixture into parts and form into several smaller balls; or, roll into one or more logs. Wrap in plastic wrap. Chill 1 hour or until firm.

3. Roll in crushed ancho chilies. Refrigerate until ready to use. Serve with crackers.

Beyond Bean Dip

Although the texture of canned beans is inferior for dishes that call for whole beans, they are simple and fast to use — especially for dips or refried bean dishes. Rinse and drain canned beans before using.

Bean layer

1	can (14 oz [398 mL]) refried beans *or* 1 can (19 oz [540 mL]) pinto beans	1
1/4 cup	sour cream	50 mL
1	jalapeno pepper, seeded and minced	1
1	clove garlic, minced	1
1 tsp	chili powder	5 mL
1/2 tsp	ground cumin	2 mL

Guacamole layer

2	ripe avocados	2
3 tbsp	lemon juice *or* lime juice	45 mL
3	green onions, minced	3
1 tsp	minced jalapeno pepper	5 mL

Garnish

1 cup	sour cream	250 mL
2	green onions, chopped	2
1	tomato, seeded and chopped	1
1 cup	shredded Cheddar cheese	250 mL
1/2 cup	sliced black olives	125 mL
	Regular and blue corn tortilla chips as accompaniments	

1. If using pinto beans, rinse and drain. Purée beans in food processor; transfer to a bowl. Stir in sour cream, jalapeno, garlic, chili powder and cumin. Set aside.

2. In another bowl, mash avocados with lemon juice. Stir in green onions and jalapeno peppers. Set aside.

3. Spread bean dip in a thin layer over a deep 12-inch (30 cm) platter. Carefully spread guacamole over bean layer. Spread with sour cream, making sure to cover guacamole completely to keep it from darkening. Starting at the outside edge of the plate, make a 2-inch (5 cm) ring of shredded cheese. Inside that ring, sprinkle green onions in a ring. Follow with black olives and finish with a pile of chopped tomato in the center of the plate. Serve with lots of regular and blue corn tortilla chips for scooping.

Chipotle Chili Butter

This combination is a favorite of Calgary caterers Gail Norton and Ellen Kelly. Use it to spread on bread, chicken or fish before grilling or, as they do, use it on jumbo shrimp that are quickly sautéed. Yum!

Canned chipotle chilies in adobo sauce are available in specialty stores and many super-markets.

2 cups	cilantro leaves	500 mL
3/4 cup	finely chopped green onions	175 mL
2	cloves garlic, minced	2
1 lb	butter, cut in pieces and softened	500 g
2 or 3	chipotle chilies packed in adobo sauce	2 or 3
1 to 2 tbsp	adobo sauce from chilies	15 to 25 mL
1 tbsp	ground cumin	15 mL
Pinch	salt	Pinch

1. In food processor, combine cilantro, green onions and garlic; pulse on and off until finely minced. Add butter, chipotle chilies, adobo sauce, cumin and salt; process until combined.

2. Store up to 2 days in the refrigerator; or, divide into smaller portions and freeze.

Cowboy Beef Jerky

Beef jerky is a cowboy classic but it's also perfect to take along in your backpack for overnight hikes.

You can also use this marinade for venison.

Instead of using the oven, dry your jerky in a home dehydrator, according to manufacturer's directions.

While you can make your own jerky, a great, preservative-free local supply can be had from Longview Meats, where Len Kirk turns out those chewy sticks you see shrink wrapped by the till at gas stations and corner stores across Alberta.

So popular and portable is the Longview Beef Jerky that local climbers hauled it up Everest during an expedition in 1994.

1 1/2 lbs	flank steak, cut along the grain into thin strips about 1/8 inch (2 mm) thick	750 g
1/2 cup	Worcestershire sauce	125 mL
1/4 cup	soy sauce	50 mL
1 tbsp	brown sugar *or* honey	15 mL
1 tsp	freshly ground black pepper	5 mL
1 tsp	seasoned salt *or* steak spice *or* seasoned meat tenderizer	5 mL
1 tsp	onion powder	5 mL
1/2 tsp	garlic powder	2 mL

1. In a zippered plastic bag, combine steak strips, Worcestershire sauce, soy sauce, brown sugar, pepper, seasoned salt, onion powder and garlic powder. Marinate overnight in refrigerator.

2. Preheat oven to its lowest setting (about 140° F [60° C]). Lift beef strips out of marinade; arrange on a wire rack on a baking sheet. Discard remaining marinade. Bake jerky with the oven door slightly ajar for 8 to 10 hours, turning beef strips once, or until dry and chewy. Check often; jerky should be dry but should bend without breaking. If it's brittle, you've cooked it too long for snacking but it can still be kept for rehydrating in soups and stews.

Prairie Oysters

Prairie oysters (or mountain oysters as they're also known) are a traditional treat during spring branding, when calves are castrated. The tender organ meat is the size of a large chicken liver and actually tastes a little like chicken livers. Testicles from grown bulls are much larger and must be sliced to 1/4-inch (5 mm) thickness before cooking — not my personal favorite.

Peeling the smaller calf testicles is time-consuming but important, unless you like your oysters chewy. One rancher told me he likes his cooked "schnitzel-style" — the meat pounded lightly to flatten before breading and frying in olive oil.

1 lb	calf testicles (about 24)	500 g
2	eggs	2
1/4 cup	milk	50 mL
1 cup	cornmeal	250 mL
1/2 cup	flour	125 mL
1/2 cup	finely crushed soda crackers (about 14 crackers)	125 mL
1 tsp	salt	5 mL
1/4 tsp	freshly ground black pepper	1 mL
1/4 tsp	cayenne pepper to taste	1 mL
	Canola oil for frying	

1. Butterfly the oysters by slicing open lengthwise without cutting completely in half. Peel off outer membrane. Cover with salted water and soak overnight in refrigerator.
2. In a bowl, beat eggs and milk until frothy. In a separate bowl, stir together cornmeal, flour, cracker crumbs, salt, pepper and cayenne pepper.
3. In a large cast iron skillet, heat about 1/2 inch (1 cm) of canola oil over medium-high heat. Drain oysters. In batches, dip in beaten egg mixture, roll in cornmeal mixture and fry in hot oil 5 minutes, turning halfway, or until golden brown and cooked through. Serve hot.

MAKES ABOUT	
18 CUPS (4.5 L)	

Spicy Salsa with Hot and Sweet Peppers

When the peppers arrive at the markets in the fall, I always put up a bunch of salsa for snacking all winter long. This is a long-standing Texas tradition, and one every cowboy would concur with.

For a milder salsa, use sweet banana, Anaheim or Cubanelle peppers, and omit hot sauce and cayenne pepper.

For hotter salsa, finish the batch with extra hot sauce or cayenne pepper to taste.

16 cups	chopped plum tomatoes (about 6 lbs [3 kg])	4 L
8 cups	chopped seeded hot banana peppers or other long, medium-hot peppers (about 2 1/2 lbs [1.25 kg])	2 L
2 cups	finely chopped seeded hot chili peppers, such as jalapeno, serrano or scotch bonnet (about 12 oz [375 g])	500 mL
4 cups	chopped onions	1 L
2 cups	cider vinegar	500 mL
1 cup	chopped red bell peppers	250 mL
1 cup	chopped yellow bell peppers	250 mL
8	cloves garlic, minced	8
2	cans (each 5 1/2 oz [156 mL]) tomato paste	2
1/4 cup	granulated sugar	50 mL
2 tbsp	salt	25 mL
4 tsp	paprika	20 mL
1 tbsp	dried oregano	15 mL
1 cup	chopped cilantro	250 mL
	Hot sauce and/or cayenne pepper to taste	

1. In a large saucepan, combine tomatoes, banana peppers, hot chili peppers, onions, cider vinegar, red and yellow peppers, garlic, tomato paste, sugar, salt. paprika and oregano. Bring to a boil, stirring often. Reduce heat to medium-low and simmer 1 to 2 hours or until salsa is thick enough to coat a spoon. Stir in cilantro; simmer 5 minutes longer.

2. Taste salsa. Season to taste with hot sauce and/or cayenne pepper. Ladle into hot, sterilized 2-cup (500 mL) Mason jars, leaving a 1/4-inch (5 mm) space at the top, and cover with 2-piece sealer lids. Process in a boiling water bath for 20 minutes.

SERVES 4

Black Bean Nachos

owboys may not have eaten nachos at the turn of the century but we certainly consume a lot of corn chips today, a testament to the spread of Tex-Mex cooking throughout the West. Today nachos have become the national snack in cowboy country. In small-town cafes, rural bars or casual city restaurants, you'll always find nachos to start a meal.

Southern Alberta is home to two of the largest corn chip makers — El Molino Foods and Del Comal Foods.

Use canned beans, rinsed and drained, or cook your own. Start with 1 cup (250 mL) dried black beans.

Salsa

2	plum tomatoes, seeded and chopped	2
1/4 cup	chopped onions	50 mL
1 tbsp	freshly squeezed lime juice	15 mL
1	jalapeno pepper, seeded and minced	1
2 tbsp	minced cilantro	25 mL
1 tbsp	chopped parsley	15 mL
1 tsp	chopped fresh thyme	5 mL
1 tsp	chopped fresh oregano	5 mL
1	green onion, chopped	1

Refried Beans

1 cup	cooked black beans	250 mL
1 tbsp	minced garlic	15 mL
2	hot chili peppers, minced	2
1/4 cup	chopped cilantro	50 mL
	Salt to taste	

Guacamole

2	ripe avocados	2
3 tbsp	freshly squeezed lime juice	45 mL
1 tsp	minced garlic	5 mL
1/4 tsp	dried thyme leaves	1 mL
1/4 tsp	dried oregano	1 mL
1	jalapeno pepper, chopped	1
12 cups	combination of yellow and blue tortilla chips	3 L
8 oz	Monterey Jack cheese, shredded	250 g

1. Salsa: In a bowl, stir together tomatoes, onions, lime juice, jalapeno, cilantro, parsley, thyme, oregano and green onion. Marinate for 1 hour in the refrigerator.

2. Refried Beans: Mash beans with a fork or purée in food processor. In a frying pan, heat olive oil over medium heat. Add mashed beans, garlic, chili peppers, and cilantro; cook for 3 minutes, stirring, or until soft and fragrant. Season with salt to taste. Set aside.

3. Guacamole: In a bowl and using a fork, mash avocado with lime juice. Stir in garlic, thyme, oregano and jalapeno. Set aside.

4. Assembly: Preheat oven to 400° F (200° C). Put tortilla chips on a large ovenproof dish. Distribute refried beans and salsa evenly over chips. Sprinkle with cheese. Bake for 5 minutes or until cheese is melted and dish is hot. Serve with guacamole on the side.

$\mathcal{S}$oup has long been a prairie pioneer tradition — old wood stoves on the farm were temperamental for baking, but a soup bone could simmer on the back of the stove all day without watching. On the ranch, it was customary to eat a large meal at noon (dinner). Then, at suppertime, mid-day leftovers could easily be recycled into soups and served with bread for the evening meal. In the summer time, gardens provided lots of vegetables for the soup pot and there was a good supply of ham hocks and soup bones for stocks when livestock was butchered. Beans, rice and barley were also staples of the soup pot, and there were always winter vegetables — like potatoes, carrots, parsnips and onions — that could be brought up from the root cellars for soups. This collection of soups ranges from old-fashioned corn chowder, split pea and bean soups to hearty soups made with regional ingredients such as wild rice and forest mushrooms. So come and get it — soup's on!

Soups

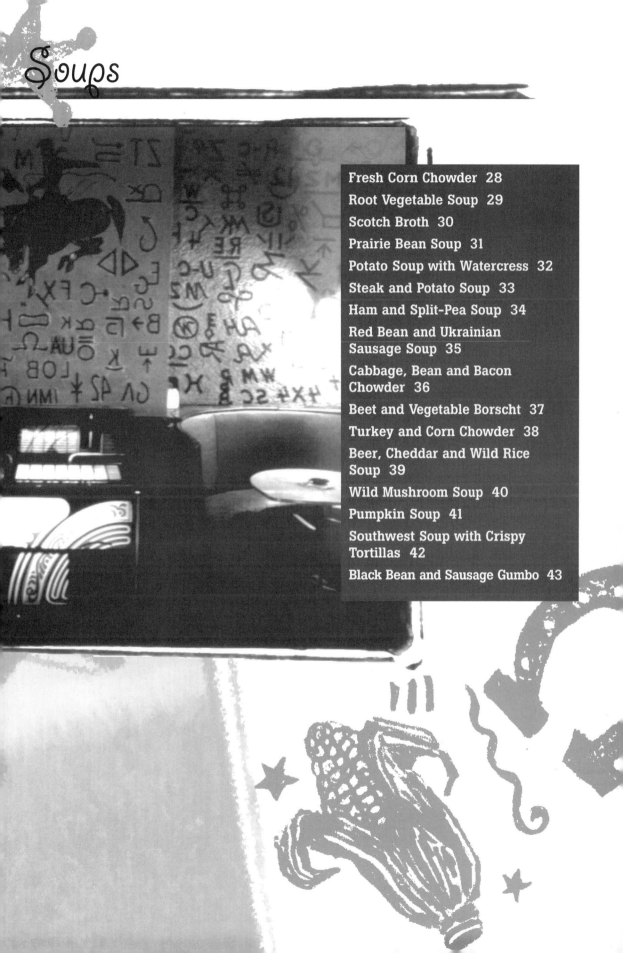

SERVES 4

Fresh Corn Chowder

orn is a staple food throughout the West, one that finds its roots with early Native tribes of the American South. The earliest explorers found corn planted in Native villages in the mid-1500s, where women used fresh corn in stews, dried it for cornmeal or boiled it with wood ashes to make hominy.

When the Taber corn stands abound in Southern Alberta in August, and you can buy a dozen cobs of fresh corn for a dollar, it's time to make this speedy corn soup. The skim milk keeps it light, too.

2	medium new red-skinned potatoes, scrubbed	2
1 tbsp	butter	15 mL
1/2 cup	chopped celery	125 mL
1 cup	chopped Bermuda, Spanish or Vidalia onion	250 mL
1 1/2 cups	fresh corn kernels or frozen corn (use frozen corn in winter months)	625 mL
1/2 tsp	salt	2 mL
1/2 tsp	dried basil	2 mL
1/4 cup	minced fresh parsley	50 mL
2 cups	skim milk	500 mL
	White pepper to taste	

1. Boil potatoes in their skins 20 minutes or until tender. Drain, saving the cooking water. Cool potatoes slightly and dice; set aside.

2. In a saucepan, melt butter over medium-high heat. Add celery and onion; cook for 3 minutes or until barely tender. Stir in corn, potatoes, salt, basil and parsley. Reduce heat to medium, cover and cook for 5 minutes or until vegetables are tender.

3. Stir in the milk and 1 cup (250 mL) of the potato cooking water. Heat gently. Season to taste with white pepper and serve immediately.

Root Vegetable Soup

*T*he flavorful root vegetables featured in this creamy soup are available throughout the year. It's a delicious combination — and very low in fat.

For a spicy garnish, soak 3 dried ancho chilies in boiling water to cover for 30 minutes. Drain, remove stems and seeds and purée chilies with 1/4 cup (50 mL) chicken stock until smooth. Combine with enough low-fat sour cream to make a creamy sauce and use to drizzle over this soup, bean soup or pumpkin soup or other creamy concoctions for a blast of chili flavor.

2 tsp	canola oil	10 mL
1	clove garlic, crushed	1
1 cup	chopped onions	250 mL
4 cups	chicken stock	1 L
1	potato, peeled and chopped	1
3/4 cup	chopped carrots	175 mL
3/4 cup	chopped peeled sweet potatoes	175 mL
1/2 cup	chopped parsnip	125 mL
2 tbsp	chopped fresh dill	25 mL

1. In a saucepan, heat oil over medium-high heat. Add onions and garlic; cook, stirring occasionally, 4 minutes or until tender. Stir in stock, potato, carrot, sweet potato and parsnip. Bring to a boil, reduce heat to medium-low and simmer, covered, for 25 to 35 minutes or until vegetables are tender.

2. Transfer soup to a blender or food processor; purée until smooth. Return to saucepan. Stir in fresh dill. Season to taste with salt and pepper.

Scotch Broth

This recipe comes from Calgary's Highlander Hotel.
It's wonderfully thick and hearty soup —
and a tribute to the Scots who first settled the Old West.

8 oz	boneless lamb shoulder or shank, trimmed of fat and finely chopped (include some meaty bones, if possible)	250 g
1	onion, diced	1
3	stalks celery, diced	3
1/2 tsp	vegetable oil	2 mL
8 cups	chicken stock	2 L
1 3/4 cups	diced white turnips (about 2)	425 mL
1 1/4 cups	diced carrots (about 3)	300 mL
1 cup	pearl barley	250 mL
2 tsp	minced garlic	10 mL
1 tsp	freshly ground black pepper	5 mL
1/2 tsp	dried thyme leaves	2 mL
	Salt to taste	

1. If you have lamb bones, combine with chopped lamb, onions, celery and oil in a shallow pan; roast in a 450° F (230° C) oven for 20 minutes or until browned and transfer to saucepan. If not, heat oil in saucepan over medium-high heat. Add onions and celery; cook 5 minutes or until starting to brown. Add the chopped lamb; cook 5 minutes, stirring occasionally, or until browned.

2. Stir in the chicken broth, turnips and carrots; bring to a boil. Reduce heat to low, cover and simmer for 15 minutes. Stir in barley, garlic, pepper and thyme; simmer, uncovered, 45 to 60 minutes or until the barley is tender and the soup is thick.

3. If using bones, remove them from the soup; add any meat from the bones back into the soup. Heat through and season to taste with salt.

SERVES 6

Prairie Bean Soup

To speed up the bean soaking process, place beans in a pot and cover with about 3 inches (7.5 cm) of cold water. Set pot over high heat and bring beans to a rolling boil. Cover the pot, remove from heat and let beans stand for 1 hour. Drain and proceed with your recipe, as if you'd soaked your beans overnight.

1 lb	Great Northern beans, soaked overnight in water to cover	500 g
3	slices smoky bacon, chopped	3
Pinch	baking soda	Pinch
2	onions, chopped	2
2	carrots, chopped	2
1	small white turnip, chopped	1
1	stalk celery, finely chopped	1
1 cup	skim milk	250 mL
	Salt and pepper to taste	
2	cloves garlic, pressed or minced	2
1 tsp	chopped fresh thyme	5 mL

1. Place drained beans in a large soup pot with 8 cups (2 L) water, bacon and baking soda. Bring to a boil, skimming scum that rises to the surface. Reduce heat and simmer, uncovered, for 45 minutes or until beans are softened. Stir in onions, carrot, turnip and celery; cook, uncovered, for 45 minutes longer or until beans and vegetables are tender.

2. Transfer one-third of the soup to a food processor or blender; purée until smooth, then return to soup pot. Add milk and heat through. Season to taste with salt and pepper. Stir in garlic and thyme and serve.

SERVES 6

Potato Soup with Watercress

atercress, which grows wild along Alberta rivers, is part of a traditional Native diet. The peppery leaves are shiny, small and round, and the plant has white flowers that grow in clusters. When you find watercress, don't uproot the plant but clip it off at the water surface.

Yukon Gold potatoes give this soup a wonderful golden color and buttery flavor.

2 tsp	olive oil	10 mL
1	yellow onion, chopped	1
6	green onions, minced	6
2 tbsp	flour	25 mL
4 cups	chicken stock	1 L
2 lbs	Yukon Gold potatoes, peeled and cut into 1/2-inch (1 cm) cubes	1 kg
1 cup	evaporated skim milk	250 mL
1	bunch watercress, stemmed and chopped	1
	Salt and pepper to taste	

1. In a saucepan heat oil over medium-high heat. Add onion and half of the green onions; cook for 3 minutes or until softened. Add stock and potatoes. Bring to a boil, reduce heat to medium and cook 10 minutes or until potatoes are tender.

2. Stir in evaporated milk and chopped watercress; cook a few minutes longer or until greens are wilted. Transfer all or part of soup to a blender or food processor; purée until smooth and return to saucepan. Season to taste with salt and pepper. Garnish with remaining green onions.

TURKEY AND CORN CHOWDER (PAGE 38) ➤

Steak and Potato Soup

This is a great way to use up leftover barbecued steak and baked potatoes, a classic steakhouse soup that's fast and easy.

1 tbsp	olive oil	15 mL
1	large onion, thinly sliced	1
2	cloves garlic, pressed	2
1	red or yellow bell pepper, sliced	1
4 cups	chopped baked potatoes with skin (about 2 baked potatoes)	1 L
2 cups	thinly sliced barbecued steak	500 mL
4 cups	beef stock *or* chicken stock	1 L
1 cup	red wine	250 mL
2 tsp	Worcestershire sauce	10 mL
	Salt and pepper to taste	
	Hot sauce to taste (optional)	

1. In a saucepan heat olive oil over medium heat. Add onion, garlic and bell pepper; cook, stirring occasionally, 8 to 10 minutes or until tender.

2. Stir in the chopped potatoes, steak, stock, wine and Worcestershire sauce. Bring to a boil, reduce heat and simmer 3 minutes. Season to taste with salt and pepper and, if desired, hot sauce.

◄ SPICY CAESAR SALAD WITH SMOKED CHICKEN AND CHILI CROUTONS (PAGE 54)

Ham and Split-Pea Soup

Lentils and split peas need no soaking and cook in 20 minutes to 1 hour, depending on the variety.

1 tbsp	butter	15 mL
1	onion, chopped	1
2	cloves garlic, minced	2
1 lb	dried split peas, rinsed	500 g
2	carrots, chopped	2
Pinch	dried thyme	Pinch
8 oz	smoked ham *or* back bacon, diced	250 g
8 cups	chicken stock	2 L
2 cups	dry white wine	500 mL
1/2 cup	brown rice	125 mL
1	package (10 oz [300 g]) frozen peas, thawed *or* equal amount of fresh garden peas, in season	1
	Salt and black pepper	

1. In a large saucepan, melt butter over medium-high heat. Add onion and garlic; cook 3 minutes or until tender. Stir in 4 cups (1 L) water, split peas, carrots, thyme, ham or back bacon, chicken stock and wine. Bring to a boil. Reduce heat to medium and cook, uncovered and stirring occasionally, for 1 hour.

2. Stir in rice, cover and simmer 45 minutes or until rice is tender. Stir in thawed peas. Season to taste with salt and pepper. Heat to boiling and serve.

Red Bean and Ukrainian Sausage Soup

Ukrainian settlers came to the Canadian prairies as early as 1901, emigrating from Russia, Austria, Poland and and other parts of Eastern Europe. Because they spoke no English, many worked as farm hands for more prosperous farmers; but soon they were cultivating their own land, with big gardens and mixed farms with cows and poultry. Their smoky garlic ham sausage is still available from Ukrainian butcher shops sprinkled throughout Western towns and cities — it's perfect for this hearty soup.

Use canned kidney beans, rinsed and drained or start with 2 cups (500 mL) dried kidney beans.

1	tomato, chopped	1
1	large onion, chopped	1
2	jalapeno peppers, seeded and chopped	2
6 oz	Ukranian sausage (kielbasa)	175 g
1 tbsp	chili powder	15 mL
1 tbsp	freshly ground black pepper	15 mL
1	bay leaf	1
2 tsp	red wine vinegar	10 mL
1	can (14 oz [398 mL]) whole stewed tomatoes, broken up	1
6 cups	beef stock	1.5 L
1/2 cup	ketchup *or* plain tomato sauce	125 mL
5 cups	cooked kidney beans	1.25 L
	Salt, granulated sugar and hot sauce to taste	

1. In a saucepan combine tomato, onion, jalapeno peppers, sausage, chili powder, pepper and bay leaf; cover and cook over medium-high heat, stirring occasionally, for 8 minutes or until tomatoes and onion have softened. Stir in vinegar. Add the stewed tomatoes, stock and ketchup; bring to a boil, reduce heat to low and simmer, uncovered, for 1 hour.

2. Stir in beans. Bring to a boil, reduce heat and simmer 10 minutes. Season to taste with salt, sugar and hot sauce.

SERVES 6

Cabbage, Bean and Bacon Chowder

The Great Northern bean is large and white, and is the North American version of the Haricot bean or Italian Cannellini bean. Substitute white kidney beans if Great Northern beans are unavailable.

2 tbsp	canola oil	25 mL
8 oz	lean Canadian back bacon, chopped	250 g
1	large onion, chopped	1
2	cloves garlic, minced	1
1	jalapeno pepper, seeded and chopped	1
2	carrots, chopped	2
1	potato, chopped	1
1	small white turnip, chopped	1
8 cups	beef stock	2 L
1 lb	green cabbage, finely shredded	500 g
1	can (19 oz [540 mL]) Great Northern beans, rinsed and drained	1
	Salt and pepper to taste	

1. In a large saucepan, heat oil over medium-high heat. Add back bacon, onion, garlic and jalapeno pepper; cook 4 minutes or until softened.

2. Stir in the carrots, potato, turnip and stock. Bring to a boil. Reduce heat to medium-low and cook, covered, for 15 to 25 minutes or until vegetables are tender.

3. Stir in cabbage and cook 15 minutes longer or until cabbage is tender. Stir in beans and heat through. Season to taste with salt and pepper.

Beet and Vegetable Borscht

Many homesteaders arrived in Alberta before World War One and, until 1930, half of the population was foreign born. Alberta's population swelled from to 374,000 in 1911 from 73,000 in 1901 , with British, German, Ukranian, French, Scandinavian, Dutch and Polish arrivals. This old-fashioned soup was popular with prairie immigrants from the Ukraine, Romania and other parts of Eastern Europe.

1 tbsp	butter	15 mL
1	large onion, minced	1
2	cloves garlic, pressed	2
3 cups	peeled and cubed potatoes	750 mL
1 cup	chopped carrots	250 mL
1	large beet, unpeeled with 1 inch (2.5 cm) of tops intact, scrubbed	1
1 3/4 cups	canned tomatoes with juices, crushed	425 mL
4 cups	shredded purple cabbage	1 L
10 cups	beef stock *or* water	2.5 L
1 tbsp	red wine vinegar	15 mL
	Salt, pepper and paprika to taste	
2 tbsp	chopped fresh dill	25 mL
1/2 cup	sour cream	125 mL
3 tbsp	all-purpose flour	45 mL

1. In a large saucepan, melt butter over medium-high heat. Add minced onion and garlic; cook 4 minutes or until starting to brown. Stir in potatoes and carrots; cook 3 minutes longer. Add the whole beet to the pot with the canned tomatoes, shredded cabbage and stock. Bring to a boil. Reduce heat to medium-low, cover and cook for 45 minutes or until beet is tender.

2. Remove beet from pot, cool slightly and slip off skin. Chop beet and return to soup. Stir in vinegar. Simmer for 10 minutes to blend flavors. Season to taste with salt, pepper and paprika. Stir in fresh dill.

3. In a small bowl, stir together sour cream and flour. Whisk into soup to thicken. Heat through but do not boil. Serve immediately.

Turkey and Corn Chowder

*H*ere's an easy soup to pull together from pantry items when you have leftover turkey or roast chicken in the freezer. Served with cornbread, it makes a pleasingly simple supper after those indulgent holiday meals are over.

1 tbsp	canola oil	15 mL
1	onion, minced	1
2	cloves garlic, minced	2
3	stalks celery, minced	3
1	red bell pepper, chopped	1
2	carrots, chopped	2
2 tsp	dried oregano	10 mL
1 1/2 tsp	ground cumin	7 mL
2	cans (each 10 oz [284 mL]) chicken stock, diluted with 2 cans of water	2
1	can (7 1/2 oz [213 mL]) tomato sauce	1
1	jalapeno pepper, seeded and minced	1
2 cups	corn	500 mL
2 cups	chopped cooked turkey	500 mL
	Salt, pepper and hot sauce to taste	
	Crushed tortilla chips *or* fried corn tortilla strips (see SOUTHWEST SOUP, page 42) as garnish	

1. In a large saucepan, heat oil over medium-high heat. Add onion, garlic, celery, red pepper and carrots; cook for 10 minutes or until tender.

2. Stir in oregano and cumin; cook, stirring, 1 minute or until spices are fragrant. Stir in stock, tomato sauce and jalapeno. Bring to a boil. Reduce heat to medium and simmer for 10 minutes.

3. Stir in turkey and corn; cook for 20 minutes longer or until carrots and corn are tender. Season to taste with hot sauce, salt and pepper. Serve garnished with crushed tortilla chips or fried corn tortilla strips.

SERVES 6

Beer, Cheddar and Wild Rice Soup

This recipe comes from the chef at Lake O'Hara Lodge, a back-country inn nestled in the Rocky Mountains near Banff. It's a hearty soup, filled with classic prairie ingredients — dark beer and wild rice.

Big Rock Traditional Ale is a good choice for this soup.

Wild and white rice mixtures are available in most supermarkets.

1 tsp	butter *or* vegetable oil	5 mL
1	onion, finely chopped	1
2	carrots, finely chopped	2
2	stalks celery, finely chopped	2
4	cloves garlic, minced	4
1 tsp	minced fresh rosemary	5 mL
2	bottles (each 12 oz [341 mL]) premium ale	2
4 cups	vegetable stock *or* chicken stock	1 L
2 to 3 cups	cooked white and wild rice	500 to 750 mL
1 cup	shredded medium or old Cheddar	250 mL
	Salt and pepper to taste	

1. In a large saucepan, melt butter over medium-high heat. Add onion, carrots and celery; cook, stirring often, 10 minutes or until starting to brown. Stir in garlic and rosemary; cook 1 minute or until fragrant.

2. Stir in the beer. Bring to a boil and cook for 1 minute, stirring up any browned bits from the bottom of the pan. Add stock and rice. Bring to a boil, reduce heat to medium and cook, uncovered, for 20 minutes.

3. Transfer one-third of the soup to a blender or food processor; purée until smooth. Return purée to the pot. Bring soup back to a boil; remove from heat. Add the cheese, stirring until it is completely melted and the soup is smooth. Season to taste with salt and pepper. Serve immediately.

Wild Mushroom Soup

Root vegetables, wild mushrooms and juniper berries flavor this richly decadent soup from Rocky Mountain chef Hubert Aumeier.

Mixed dried wild mushrooms can be purchased from specialty and health food stores. They're expensive, but make an incredibly elegant soup.

3 tbsp	butter	45 mL
1	small white turnip, diced	1
1	onion, diced	1
3	potatoes, peeled and chopped	3
6	cloves garlic, minced	6
1	leek, white part only, chopped	1
1/2 cup	sherry	125 mL
3	juniper berries	3
	Bouquet garni (2 bay leaves with a piece of carrot, celery and parsley, tied together with string)	
2 cups	dried mixed wild mushrooms	500 mL
12 cups	chicken stock	3 L
4 cups	heavy (35%) cream	1 L
	Salt and pepper to taste	

1. Soak mushrooms in 2 cups (500 mL) warm water for 20 minutes or until softened. Drain, reserving soaking liquid. Chop mushrooms. Set aside.

2. In a stock pot, melt butter over medium-high heat. Add turnip, onion, potatoes, garlic and leek; cook for 10 minutes, stirring constantly, or until golden. Stir in the sherry. Add the juniper berries, *bouquet garni*, mushrooms, mushroom soaking liquid and chicken stock. Bring to a boil; boil until liquid has been reduced by one-third or to about 8 cups (2 L).

3. Stir in the cream and return to a boil. Remove immediately from heat and cool. Remove *bouquet garni*. In batches, transfer to a food processor or blender; purée until smooth. Season to taste with salt and pepper. To serve, reheat gently until piping hot.

Pumpkin Soup

If you have fresh pumpkin, you can simply peel and cube it and add it to the pot along with the carrots and potatoes. Then purée the whole thing when all of the vegetables are tender.

Canned pumpkin is widely available — do not confuse it with canned pumpkin pie filling, which contains spices and oil.

1/4 cup	butter	50 mL
2	large onions, chopped	2
1	stalk celery, chopped	1
2	leeks, white part only, chopped	2
3	large carrots, chopped	3
3	large potatoes, chopped	3
6 cups	chicken stock	1.5 L
2 cups	canned pumpkin	500 mL
1 1/2 cups	cream *or* evaporated milk	375 mL
	Salt and pepper to taste	
2 tbsp	butter	25 mL
1/4 cup	chopped green onions	50 mL
1/4 cup	chopped fresh parsley	50 mL

1. In a large saucepan, melt butter over medium-high heat. Add onions and celery; cook for 5 minutes or until tender. Stir in leeks, carrots and potato; cook, stirring occasionally, for 5 minutes longer.

2. Add chicken stock. Bring to a boil, reduce heat to medium and cook, uncovered, for 25 to 35 minutes or until vegetables are tender. Cool slightly. Transfer solid chunks with some of the broth to a blender or food processor; purée until smooth.

3. Return purée to saucepan along with pumpkin and cream. Heat through but do not boil. Season to taste with salt and pepper. Whisk in butter until melted; stir in green onions and parsley. Serve immediately.

Southwest Soup with Crispy Tortillas

This delicious Mexican-inspired soup is served through-out the West, from New Mexico to Medicine Hat. It's light and tasty — and very easy when you want something fast and unusual!

1/2 cup	vegetable oil	125 mL
3	corn tortillas, cut into strips	3
4 cups	chicken stock	1 L
1	plum tomato, seeded and finely chopped	1
2 tbsp	lime juice	25 mL
5	drops hot sauce	5
	Salt and pepper	
8 oz	boneless skinless chicken breast, cut into thin strips	250 g
1	avocado, peeled and chopped	1
1/2 cup	shredded Monterey Jack cheese	125 mL
2	green onions, chopped	2

1. In a frying pan, heat oil over medium-high heat. In batches, cook tortilla strips 2 minutes or until golden and crispy; drain on paper towels. Set aside.

2. In a saucepan combine chicken stock, tomato and lime juice. Bring to a boil. Reduce heat to medium-low. Stir in hot sauce. Season to taste with salt and pepper. Stir in chicken strips; cook for 2 minutes or until just cooked through.

3. Divide the tortilla strips, avocado chunks and shredded cheese evenly among four soup bowls. Ladle the hot broth and chicken over top. Garnish each serving with some of the chopped green onions.

Black Bean and Sausage Gumbo

This hearty soup is really almost a stew. Serve it as a main course with cornbread and beer or ladle it over hot cooked rice in deep soup plates.

Use canned black beans, rinsed and drained, or start with 2 cups (500 mL) dried black beans.

1/2 cup	canola oil	125 mL
1/2 cup	all-purpose flour	125 mL
4	onions, chopped	4
4	stalks celery, chopped	4
1	red bell pepper, chopped	1
6	cloves garlic, pressed	6
8 cups	chicken stock	2 L
5 cups	cooked black beans	1.25 L
1/4 cup	Worcestershire sauce	50 mL
2 lbs	spicy Italian sausages, cooked and sliced	1 kg
1/2 tsp	chopped fresh thyme	2 mL
	Salt and pepper to taste	
1/2 cup	minced fresh parsley	125 mL
1/2 cup	chopped green onions	125 mL
1/2 cup	seeded and chopped tomatoes	125 mL
	Cornbread or hot cooked rice as accompaniment	

1. In a stock pot, cook oil and flour over medium heat, stirring constantly, for 10 minutes or until you have a brown *roux* the color of peanut butter. Be careful, this gets very hot and burns easily.

2. Stir in onions, celery, red pepper and garlic; cook, covered, for 8 minutes, stirring occasionally, or until vegetables are tender. Stir in stock, beans, Worcestershire sauce, sausage and thyme. Bring to a boil, reduce heat to medium-low and cook, covered, for 30 minutes. Season to taste with salt and pepper. Stir in parsley and green onions. Place a mound of hot cooked rice in each serving bowl and spoon gumbo over top. Serve garnished with tomatoes.

Salads were unheard of in the Old West except during the summertime, when wild dandelion greens, watercress and garden lettuce was available. 🐎 Still, a good potato salad is about as Western as apple pie and if you ask for guests to bring a salad to a potluck, you'll probably get at least three made with potatoes and mayonnaise. 🐎 These days, main meal and side salads are as popular on the prairies as anywhere else in America, even in cowboy kitchens. While I've steered away from the ubiquitous jellied salad (so popular with prairie cooks a generation ago), you can't talk about country cowboy cooking without mentioning bean salad or buttermilk dressing. 🐎 And, of course, there are several recipes here for coleslaw — a mainstay salad, even in the early days, because it was made from cabbage and carrots (vegetables that could be stored for part of the winter in the cellar). Today coleslaw is as popular as ever, served with burgers, fish and chips, and sandwiches everywhere. And at least one of these versions of the popular cabbage salad turns up at every Stampede barbecue, the perfect vegetable dish on any beef-and-beans menu. 🐎 This collection of salad recipes includes some old favorites and some updated variations on indigenous themes — like the ever-popular Caesar salad, modernized here with smoked chicken and chili croutons. 🐎 So c'mon everybody — eat your greens!

Salads

New Potato Salad

otato salad is a mainstay of prairie cooking. In the early summer, there's nothing quite like the flavor of baby potatoes in your salad, tiny tubers quickly collected from around the surface of growing plants. In the winter, use waxy red potatoes for a great salad that's almost as wonderful as its fresh summer counterpart.

When fresh garden peas are available, shell them and add them raw to your potato salad for sweet crunchy flavor and great color.

2 lbs	small new potatoes, scrubbed	1 kg
1/2 cup	reduced-fat mayonnaise	125 mL
1/2 cup	low-fat sour cream or yogurt	125 mL
1 tbsp	Dijon or herb mustard	15 mL
1 tbsp	minced fresh dill (or 1 tsp [5 mL] dried)	15 mL
1 tbsp	fresh lemon juice	15 mL
	Salt and pepper to taste	
1/2 cup	chopped celery	125 mL
1/3 cup	chopped green onions	75 mL
3	hard-boiled eggs, chopped	3
6	radishes, sliced (optional)	6
1/2 cup	freshly shelled peas (optional)	125 mL

1. Steam potatoes in their skins until tender. Cool potatoes slightly; halve or chop into big bite-sized chunks.

2. In a bowl, whisk together mayonnaise, sour cream, mustard, dill, lemon juice and salt and pepper to taste.

3. In a large bowl, toss warm potatoes with dressing. Add celery, green onions, hard-boiled eggs and, if using, radishes and peas. Toss carefully, trying to keep the potatoes intact. Chill or serve immediately as a warm salad.

Black Bean and Rice Salad

This colorful salad makes a great summer meal or portable potluck offering. It's also very Western with Tex-Mex overtones and earthy black beans.

1 cup	dried black beans, soaked overnight in water to cover	250 mL
1	onion, halved	1
2	cloves garlic, chopped	2
1	small carrot	1
1	sprig fresh parsley	1
1 cup	white rice	250 mL
1 tbsp	canola oil	15 mL
1 tsp	turmeric	5 mL
1/2 tsp	ground cumin	2 mL
1/2 tsp	salt	2 mL

Dressing

3 tbsp	olive oil	45 mL
3 tbsp	fresh lime juice	45 mL
1/2 tsp	ground cumin	2 mL
2	tomatoes, seeded and diced	2
1	small red onion, diced	1
1	red bell pepper, diced	1
1	jalapeno pepper, seeded and minced	1
1/4 cup	chopped cilantro	50 mL
	Cayenne pepper to taste	

1. In a saucepan combine drained beans with 8 cups (2 L) cold water, onion, garlic, carrot and parsley. Bring to a boil. Reduce heat and simmer 1 1/2 hours or until tender. Drain and cool. Discard onion, carrot and parsley.

2. Meanwhile, in a small saucepan combine 1 3/4 cups (425 mL) cold water, rice, oil, turmeric, cumin and 1/2 tsp (2 mL) salt. Bring to a boil, cover, reduce heat to low and simmer 30 minutes. Fluff rice and cool to room temperature.

3. Make the dressing: In a small bowl, whisk together olive oil, lime juice and cumin. Set aside.

4. In a large bowl, toss cooled beans and rice with tomatoes, red onion, red pepper, jalapenos, cilantro and dressing. Season to taste with cayenne pepper and salt. Chill.

Fresh Corn and Greens with Crispy Tortillas

Imagine this southern-inspired salad to start an elegant Western meal of barbecue beef or prime rib. On its own, it makes a great luncheon or light summer salad, perfect paired with quesadillas.

We may only see dandelions as lawn pests to be sought out and destroyed, but prairie homesteaders ate them — leaves, roots, flowers and all. Toss the slightly bitter young greens in salads for a flavor contrast and roast the cleaned roots in the oven until crisp to use as a substitute for coffee.

1 1/2 cups	fresh corn kernels (from about 3 ears of corn)	375 mL
1 cup	diced kohlrabi *or* jicama	250 mL
2	tomatoes, seeded and chopped	2
1	avocado, chopped	1
1	red pepper, chopped	1
1 cup	canola oil for frying	250 mL
6	corn tortillas, cut into 1/4-inch (5 mm) strips	6
1 lb	mixed greens (including dandelions, if available), cleaned and torn	500 g

Dressing

1/4 cup	olive oil	50 mL
1/4 cup	wine vinegar	50 mL
3 tbsp	minced cilantro	45 mL
2 tsp	soy sauce	10 mL
2 tsp	orange juice	10 mL
1 tsp	granulated sugar	5 mL
1 tsp	dry mustard	5 mL
2	green onions, chopped	2
1	dried chili, crushed	1
	Salt and pepper to taste	

1. In a frying pan, heat canola oil over medium-high heat. In batches, cook tortilla strips for 2 minutes, stirring occasionally, or until golden and crispy. Drain on paper towels. Set aside.

2. In a bowl, combine corn, kohlrabi or jicama, tomato, avocado and pepper. Set aside.

3. In a blender or food processor, combine olive oil, wine vinegar, cilantro, soy sauce, orange juice, sugar, mustard, green onions and chili. Purée until smooth. Toss dressing with corn-avocado salad. Season to taste with salt and pepper.

4. Arrange greens on individual salad plates. Top with a scoop of corn salad. Sprinkle each salad with tortilla strips.

Potluck Bean and Pasta Salad

ean salads and macaroni salads are standard fare at western hoe-downs and prairie picnics. Here's a recipe that combines the best of both with a few new twists, a favorite of mine for summer barbecues and potluck dinners.

For convenience, use 1 can (14 oz [398 mL]) kidney beans and 1 can (14 oz [398 mL]) chickpeas, rinsed and drained.

Dressing

2 tbsp	red wine vinegar	25 mL
1 tbsp	fresh lemon juice	15 mL
1 tbsp	Dijon mustard	15 mL
2 tsp	Worcestershire sauce	10 mL
1 tsp	granulated sugar	5 mL
1/2 tsp	salt	2 mL
1/4 tsp	freshly ground black pepper	1 mL
2	cloves garlic	2
1/2 cup	extra virgin olive oil	125 mL
2 tbsp	minced fresh parsley	25 mL
1 tbsp	basil pesto *or* minced fresh basil	15 mL
3 cups	short pasta (small shells, rotini or radiatore)	750 mL
1 1/2 cups	cooked kidney beans	375 mL
1 1/2 cups	cooked chickpeas	375 mL
1 cup	diced yellow peppers	250 mL
1/2 cup	sliced black olives	125 mL
3	large plum tomatoes, seeded and chopped	3
Half	red onion, diced	Half
	Salt and pepper to taste	

1. Make the dressing: In a small glass measuring cup, whisk together vinegar, lemon juice, mustard, Worcestershire sauce, sugar, salt and pepper; set aside. In a food processor, chop garlic. Add vinegar mixture and process until well mixed. With machine running, slowly pour olive oil, parsley and pesto through feed tube. Set aside.

2. In a large pot of boiling, salted water, cook pasta for 8 to 10 minutes or until *al dente*; drain. Rinse under cold running water; drain again, shaking well to remove any excess water.

3. In a large bowl, toss together pasta, kidney beans, chickpeas and dressing. Add yellow peppers, olives, chopped tomatoes and red onions. Chill well. Season to taste with salt and pepper.

Spinach and Summer Greens with Spicy Buttermilk Dressing

ative people enjoyed various types of greens, from wild mallow and sorrel to lamb's quarters, cooked or fresh, long before wild greens became trendy. It's easy to collect greens in the wild or to grow these "weeds" in the backyard to augment summer salads.

6 cups	torn mixed salad greens (romaine, spinach, watercress, butter lettuce)	1.5 L
1 cup	cherry tomatoes, halved	250 mL
1/4 cup	sliced green onions	50 mL
6	radishes, slivered	6

Dressing

1 cup	buttermilk	250 mL
1/2 cup	medium salsa	125 mL
1/3 cup	light mayonnaise	75 mL
2 tbsp	chopped fresh parsley	25 mL
1/2 tsp	granulated sugar	2 mL
1/2 tsp	dried dill	2 mL
1/4 tsp	dry mustard	1 mL
Pinch	white pepper	Pinch
	Salt to taste	

1. In a large bowl, gently toss together salad greens, tomatoes, green onions and radishes. Set aside.

2. Make the dressing: In a food processor combine buttermilk, salsa, mayonnaise, parsley, sugar, dill, mustard and pepper; process until combined and almost smooth. (Makes 2 cups [500 mL].) Drizzle half of the dressing over the salad; toss to coat. Season to taste with salt. Refrigerate remaining dressing.

Coleslaw with Old-Fashioned Boiled Dressing

SERVES 6 TO 8

This is an old-fashioned dressing, probably the only one in most prairie farm repertoires until the advent of bottled Ranch, Caesar and Thousand Island varieties. It's great on cabbage salad, mixed greens, fresh tomatoes — even cooked potatoes. It keeps in a jar in the refrigerator for 2 weeks.

1 cup	granulated sugar	250 mL
3 tbsp	flour	45 mL
4 tsp	dry mustard	20 mL
1 tsp	salt	5 mL
1 cup	buttermilk *or* skim milk	250 mL
1	egg *or* 2 egg yolks, beaten	1
1 cup	cider vinegar	250 mL
2 tbsp	butter	25 mL
1	small head green cabbage (about 2 lbs [1 kg]), finely shredded	1
1	red apple, grated and cored but not peeled	1
4	green onions, chopped	4
2	carrots, grated	2
	Salt and pepper to taste	

1. In a bowl set over (not in) a saucepan of boiling water, stir together sugar, flour, mustard and salt. Whisk in buttermilk and beaten egg until smooth. Slowly whisk in vinegar; cook, stirring constantly, for 8 minutes or until dressing is thick. Remove bowl from saucepan. Stir in butter until melted. Cover and refrigerate. Makes 2 1/2 cups (625 mL).

2. In a large bowl, combine shredded cabbage, apple, green onions and carrots with 1 1/4 cups (300 mL) of the boiled dressing or enough to moisten. Toss well to coat. Season with salt and pepper. Chill.

Colorful Summer Slaw

Light, refreshing and low in fat, here's coleslaw that's made without the usual mayonnaise.

2 cups	shredded red cabbage	500 mL
2 cups	shredded green cabbage	500 mL
1 cup	shredded carrots	250 mL
3	green onions, chopped	3
Dressing		
1/4 cup	white vinegar	50 mL
2 tsp	granulated sugar	10 mL
3/4 tsp	salt	4 mL
1/2 tsp	freshly ground black pepper	2 mL
1/2 tsp	dry mustard	2 mL
1	clove garlic, minced	1
1/4 cup	vegetable oil	50 mL

1. In a large bowl, toss together cabbage, carrots and green onions.
2. In a small bowl, whisk together vinegar, sugar, salt, pepper, mustard and garlic. Slowly whisk in the oil until emulsified. Pour dressing over salad; toss to coat.

Deli-Style Coleslaw

Here's a coleslaw that's silky rather than crunchy. This popular deli-style recipe comes from Cafe Metro in Calgary. The recipe is large enough to feed a Stampede party crowd and the salad pairs perfectly with a big corned beef on rye sandwich.

1	large green cabbage (about 4 lbs [2 kg]), finely shredded	1
1	large onion, shredded	1
2	carrots, shredded	2
1 cup	granulated sugar	250 mL
1 tsp	salt	5 mL
Dressing		
1 1/4 cups	white vinegar	300 mL
1 cup	vegetable oil	250 mL
1/3 cup	granulated sugar	75 mL
4 tsp	celery seed	20 mL
1 tbsp	prepared mustard	15 mL

1. In a large bowl, toss together cabbage, onion, carrots, sugar and salt. Set aside.
2. In a small saucepan, combine vinegar, vegetable oil, sugar, celery seed and mustard. Bring to a boil; pour hot dressing over salad vegetables. Mix well. Chill overnight.

SERVES 8

Smoked Turkey and Cracked Wheat Salad

moked turkey adds special flavor to this salad but it's also worth trying with the leftover turkey from your holiday bird.

1 cup	bulgar *or* coarse cracked wheat	250 mL
1/2 cup	dried mushrooms	125 mL

Vinaigrette

1/4 cup	olive oil	50 mL
2 tbsp	wine vinegar	25 mL
1 tsp	minced ginger root	5 mL
1 tsp	soy sauce	5 mL
1/2 tsp	salt	2 mL
1/4 tsp	hot sauce or hot chili paste	1 mL
1	clove garlic, minced	1
8 oz	smoked turkey or chicken, diced	250 g
3/4 cup	chopped toasted pecans	175 mL
3	green onions, chopped	3
1	small red bell pepper, chopped	1
1	small yellow pepper, chopped	1
	Lettuce leaves	

1. In a saucepan bring 2 cups (500 mL) water to a boil. Stir in bulgar, cover, remove from heat and let stand 20 minutes to soften. Drain and cool.

2. Soak dried mushrooms in hot water to cover for 20 minutes or until softened. Drain. Remove and discard stems; cut caps into slivers. Set aside.

3. Make the vinaigrette: In a small bowl, whisk together olive oil, vinegar, ginger, soy sauce, salt, hot sauce and garlic. Set aside.

4. In a bowl, combine bulgar, mushrooms, smoked turkey, pecans, green onions and peppers. Pour dressing over salad; toss to coat. Chill. Serve salad on individual lettuce leaves.

Spicy Caesar Salad with Smoked Chicken and Chili Croutons

Here's the perfect recipe for anyone who's tired of the traditional Caesar. This salad's a meal in itself!

Green pumpkin seeds, or pepitas, *are available in health food stores.*

PREHEAT OVEN TO 350° F (180° C)
BAKING SHEET

Dressing

1	large head garlic	1
1 tsp	olive oil	5 mL
1 tbsp	ground cumin	15 mL
2 tsp	ground coriander	10 mL
3	anchovy filets, chopped	3
2	large egg yolks	2
1 tbsp	Dijon mustard	15 mL
1 tbsp	Worcestershire sauce	15 mL
2 tsp	balsamic vinegar	10 mL
1 tsp	hot sauce	5 mL
3/4 cup	canola oil	175 mL
3/4 cup	light olive oil	175 mL
3	jalapeno peppers, roasted, peeled, seeded and chopped	3
3 tbsp	fresh lime juice	45 mL
2 tbsp	chopped cilantro	25 mL

Croutons

2 cups	cubed French bread	500 mL
3 tbsp	olive oil	45 mL
1 tbsp	chili powder	15 mL
1	large head romaine lettuce, washed and torn into bite-sized pieces	1
1/3 cup	grated Parmesan cheese	75 mL
1/3 cup	cooked black beans	75 mL
1 cup	shredded smoked chicken *or* leftover barbecued chicken	250 mL
1/4 cup	hulled green pumpkin seeds, toasted	50 mL
1/4 cup	crumbled goat cheese *or* feta	50 mL
	Halved red and/or yellow cherry tomatoes to garnish	

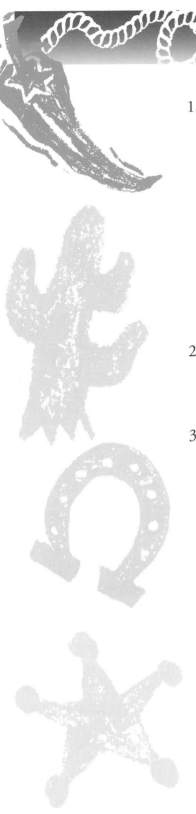

1. Make dressing: Drizzle garlic with 1 tsp (5 mL) olive oil, wrap garlic loosely in foil and bake for 30 minutes or until soft. Cool slightly, then squeeze out roasted garlic from cloves. Meanwhile, in a small frying pan, cook cumin and coriander over medium-high heat for 1 minute or until fragrant. In food processor combine garlic pulp, toasted spices, anchovies and egg yolks; process until well mixed. Add mustard, Worcestershire, balsamic vinegar and hot sauce; pulse to mix well. With machine running, add oil through the feed tube in a slow, steady stream until a thick sauce forms. Stir in roasted jalapenos, lime juice and cilantro. Chill. Makes 2 1/4 cups (550 mL).

2. Make croutons: Toss bread cubes with oil and chili powder. Spread in a single layer on baking sheet. Bake for 10 to 12 minutes, turning occasionally, or until crisp. Do not overcook or the chili powder will become bitter. Set aside.

3. In a large bowl, toss lettuce, Parmesan, black beans and 1 cup (250 mL) of the dressing until well-mixed. Divide salad mixture among salad plates. Sprinkle each with some of the smoked chicken, pumpkin seeds and crumbled goat cheese. Decorate each salad with cherry tomatoes and chili croutons.

very ranch in the Old West had chickens and every week most farm families would find at least one chicken in the pot. For soups, stews, roasted and fried chicken, there was always a source of fresh poultry for the cowboy cook on the ranch. ⚞ While cowboys couldn't count on a chicken dinner on the open range, a lucky Cookie might shoot a prairie chicken or grouse or bag a few pheasants for a special meal during a roundup. Even pigeons were found on early prairie plates, as was the occasional partridge. Back at the ranch there was always a chicken coop for birds and eggs, and often a supply of fresh turkeys, too. ⚞ These days there are lots of chickens and turkeys produced on the prairies, plus supplies of more exotic birds like pheasant, duck and quail. ⚞ The newest bird on the Alberta horizon has a huge leg up on these finer domestic fowl — many ranchers are now replacing at least some of their cattle herds with ostrich, a mega bird on the hoof that requires much less land to produce than their bovine counterparts.

Poultry

SERVES 4 TO 6

Chicken Pot Pie with Cornmeal Dumplings

On a cattle drive, one of the most hallowed members of the team was the cook, or "cookie," as he was often dubbed. Known as one of the hardest working members of the roundup team, the chuckwagon cook was up before dawn cooking up beans and biscuits, baked bread and pies in a cast-iron dutch oven. He even mended clothes, mediated disputes and administered emergency medicine.

Stew

2 tbsp	butter	25 mL
1 tbsp	canola oil	15 mL
3 lbs	boneless skinless chicken thighs, quartered	1.5 kg
1	large onion, minced	1
2	cloves garlic, minced	2
1 tbsp	all-purpose flour	15 mL
3	carrots, diced	3
3	stalks celery, diced	3
1	parsnip, diced	1
1	small turnip, diced	1
1 cup	chicken stock	250 mL
1/2 cup	dry white wine or sherry	125 mL
1	bay leaf	1
2 tbsp	chopped fresh parsley	25 mL
1/4 tsp	dried thyme leaves	1 mL
1/4 tsp	dried sage	1 mL
	Salt and pepper to taste	

Dumplings

1/2 cup	cornmeal	125 mL
1/2 cup	all-purpose flour	125 mL
1 1/2 tsp	baking powder	7 mL
1/2 tsp	salt	2 mL
1	egg, beaten	1
1/3 cup	milk	75 mL
1 tbsp	melted butter	15 mL
1/2 tsp	Dijon mustard	2 mL

1. Stew: In a Dutch oven, heat butter and oil over medium-high heat. In batches, cook chicken pieces for 5 minutes, turning occasionally, or until browned. Set chicken aside. Discard all but 1 tbsp (15 mL) of fat in the pan. Cook onion 2 minutes, stirring. Stir in garlic; cook 1 minute longer. Stir in flour until well-mixed. Stir in carrot, celery, parsnip, turnip, stock, wine and bay leaf.

2. Bring to a boil, stirring and scraping browned bits off the bottom of the pan. Return browned chicken and juices to pan, reduce heat to low, cover and cook for 30 to 45 minutes or until chicken is cooked through. Discard bay leaf. Season with parsley, thyme, sage, and salt and pepper to taste.

3. Dumplings: In a bowl, stir together cornmeal, flour, baking powder and salt. In another bowl, whisk together egg, milk, butter and mustard. Make a well in the center of dry mixture; pour in wet ingredients and mix to combine. When the stew is cooked, spoon the dumplings on top, cover the pot and simmer until firm, about 15 minutes. Alternatively, place the stew in a casserole dish, top with cornmeal mixture and bake uncovered at 425° F (220° C) for 15 to 20 minutes or until top is golden.

Roast Chicken with Ham and Mushroom Dressing

Some chuckwagon cooks were green horns, others were ropers too old to ride but too hooked on the cowboy life to stay on the farm. A good cook could keep an outfit running smoothly — a bad one could incite a mutiny — and while some commanded respect, others gained nothing but scorn. The names given to the cowboy cook provides some clue — nicknames from Soggy and Cold Bread Joe to slang monickers like bean master, belly cheater, biscuit roller, grub worm and old lady.

PREHEAT OVEN TO 450° F (230° C)
SHALLOW ROASTING PAN WITH RACK

3 tbsp	butter, divided	45 mL
1	onion, chopped	1
1	clove garlic, minced	1
3 cups	chopped mushrooms (about 8 oz [250 g])	750 mL
4 cups	fresh whole grain bread crumbs (about half a loaf)	1 L
1/2 cup	cubed cooked ham or cubed cooked back bacon	125 mL
1/4 cup	minced fresh parsley	50 mL
1/2 tsp	ground sage	2 mL
1/2 tsp	dried thyme leaves	2 mL
	Salt and pepper to taste	
1	chicken, preferably free range (about 5 to 7 lbs [2.5 to 3.5 kg])	1
2 tbsp	all-purpose flour	25 mL
1/2 cup	chicken stock	125 mL
1/2 cup	white wine	125 mL

1. In a frying pan, melt 2 tbsp (25 mL) of the butter over medium-high heat. Cook onion and garlic 3 minutes or until tender. Stir in mushrooms; cook 4 minutes or until most of the liquid is gone. Transfer to a bowl. Stir in bread crumbs, ham, parsley, sage and thyme. Season to taste with salt and pepper. Set aside.

2. Remove giblets and neck from chicken. Stuff loosely. Tuck wings under back. Truss chicken or tie legs together. Place any remaining stuffing in a casserole dish; cover and add to oven during last 30 minutes of roasting time. Place chicken breast side up on rack in roasting pan. Rub with remaining butter. Roast for 15 minutes. Reduce heat to 350° F (180° C) and roast 2 to 2 1/2 hours, basting occasionally, or until juices run clear when chicken is pierced and meat thermometer reads 185° F (85° C) inserted in thickest part of thigh and 165° F (75° C) inserted in stuffing. Remove bird to platter and tent with foil to keep warm. Let rest 10 minutes before carving.

3. Meanwhile, pour pan juices into a small saucepan and set over medium-high heat. Whisk in flour; cook for 1 minute, stirring. Whisk in chicken stock and white wine. Cook 5 minutes or until smooth and bubbly. Season to taste with salt and pepper. Pass gravy with chicken and stuffing.

Grilled Chicken with Tequila Tomato Sauce

You can substitute turkey cutlets for the chicken. Marinate and grill quickly over high heat, about 2 to 3 minutes per side, until just cooked through. The spicy sauce used here is also good with other grilled meats.

6	chicken breasts (about 4 lbs [2 kg])	6
1 tbsp	olive oil	15 mL
1 tbsp	fresh lime juice	15 mL
1/2 tsp	ground cumin	2 mL
1/4 tsp	chili powder *or* cayenne pepper	1 mL

Sauce

1 tbsp	olive oil	15 mL
1	large onion, chopped	1
1 cup	chopped fresh or canned tomatoes	250 mL
1 cup	chicken stock	250 mL
1/2 cup	gold tequila	125 mL
1 tsp	dried oregano	5 mL
1	red or yellow bell pepper, roasted, peeled and seeded	1
1	rehydrated chipotle chili, seeded and chopped *or* 1 canned chipotle chili	1
2 tbsp	fresh lime juice	25 mL
1 tsp	granulated sugar	5 mL
2	cloves garlic, pressed	2
	Salt to taste	
	Cornbread, grilled polenta or cooked rice as accompaniment	

1. Skin chicken breasts and place in a shallow glass dish. In a small bowl, whisk together olive oil, lime juice, cumin and chili powder; pour over chicken. Cover. Refrigerate for 2 hours, turning occasionally.

2. In a saucepan, heat oil over medium heat. Cook onions 3 minutes or until softened. Stir in tomatoes, chicken stock, tequila and oregano. Bring to a boil, reduce heat to medium and simmer, uncovered, for 20 minutes.

3. In a food processor, combine roasted pepper, chipotle, lime juice, sugar and garlic; purée until smooth. Add tomato sauce; process until very smooth. Return to pan and simmer sauce a few minutes or until thickened slightly. Season to taste with salt. Keep warm.

4. Meanwhile, bring chicken to room temperature. Grill over medium hot coals or gas flame until cooked through, about 15 minutes in total. Serve chicken in a pool of the tequila tomato sauce with cornbread, grilled polenta or rice.

Chicken Breast with Bread Stuffing

PREHEAT OVEN TO 400° F (200° C)
9 BY 13-INCH (3 L) BAKING DISH

Here's a recipe that delivers all the flavor of a full-fledged roast chicken or turkey dinner in a simple dinner for six.

Mince vegetables for the sauce in a food processor to save time.

Stuffing

1 tbsp	canola oil	15 mL
2	stalks celery, finely chopped	2
1	small onion, chopped	1
4	slices day-old bread (preferably a grainy bread), cubed	4
2 tbsp	milk	25 mL
1 tsp	ground sage	5 mL
1/2 tsp	celery salt	2 mL
1/2 tsp	ground thyme	2 mL
1	pear, peeled, cored and chopped	1

Sauce

1 tsp	canola oil	5 mL
1	carrot, minced	1
1	stalk celery, minced	1
1	clove garlic, minced	1
1 cup	orange juice	250 mL
1 cup	chicken stock	250 mL
1 tsp	ground sage	5 mL
1/2 tsp	ground thyme	2 mL
1 tbsp	cornstarch	15 mL
6	large, boneless chicken breast halves, with skin (about 4 lbs [2 kg])	6
	Olive oil	
	Paprika	

1. **Stuffing:** In a frying pan, heat oil over medium-high heat. Cook celery and onion 5 minutes or until tender. Stir in bread cubes, milk, sage, celery salt, thyme and pear. Set aside

Recipe continues...

CHICKEN POT PIE WITH CORNMEAL DUMPLINGS (PAGE 58)
OVERLEAF, FROM LOWER LEFT: COWBOY BEEF JERKY (PAGE 21)
BEYOND BEAN DIP (PAGE 19); SPICY SALSA WITH HOT AND SWEET PEPPERS (PAGE 23)

2. Sauce: In a saucepan, heat oil over medium heat. Add carrot, celery and garlic; cook, stirring often, 10 minutes or until tender. Stir in orange juice, chicken stock, sage and thyme. Bring to a boil; boil until reduced by one-quarter. In a small bowl, stir cornstarch with 1 tbsp (15 mL) cold water until smooth; whisk into sauce. Simmer sauce until thickened. Keep warm.

3. Remove skin from chicken breasts, setting skin aside. Between two sheets of waxed paper, pound each breast to an even thickness. Divide stuffing into 6 equal portions. With your hands, compress a portion of stuffing into a ball and place in the middle of a chicken breast. Draw edges of chicken up to enclose filling; stretch a piece of reserved skin over the top and down the sides. Place chicken roll skin-side up in baking dish. Repeat with remaining stuffing and breasts.

4. Brush chicken packets with olive oil and sprinkle with paprika. Cover dish tightly with foil. Bake for 25 minutes. Remove cover; bake 20 minutes longer or until skin is crispy and chicken is cooked through. Serve with sauce.

◄ GRILLED CHICKEN WITH TEQUILA TOMATO SALSA (PAGE 62)

Harvest Chicken Stew

In the fall, farmer's markets are bursting with colorful peppers and tomatoes. Check the markets or your favorite small butcher for double-smoked bacon, too. It adds special flavor to this portable stew, which may even be better when cooked ahead and reheated.

1 tbsp	olive oil	15 mL
1 tbsp	butter	15 mL
4	slices bacon (preferably double-smoked), julienned	4
8	cloves garlic, peeled	8
4 lbs	chicken pieces, skinned *or* 2 to 3 lbs (1 to 1.5 kg) skinless boneless chicken thighs, halved	2 kg
2 tbsp	red wine	25 mL
2 tbsp	brandy or cognac	25 mL
1 cup	white wine	250 mL
1	carrot, peeled	1
1	bay leaf	1
1	sprig fresh parsley	1
3	ripe tomatoes, seeded and chopped *or* 1 small can (14 oz [398 mL]) tomatoes, crushed)	3
2	onions, quartered and sliced	2
1	red bell pepper, roasted, peeled and cut into strips	1
1	yellow bell pepper, roasted, peeled and cut into strips	1
1	green bell pepper, roasted, peeled and cut into strips	1
1 or 2	jalapeno peppers, seeded and minced	1 or 2
	Salt and pepper to taste	
	Beurre manie (equal amounts of soft butter and flour combined) or cornstarch for thickening (optional)	
	GARLIC MASHED SPUDS (see recipe, page 137) as an accompaniment	

1. In a large Dutch oven, heat oil and butter over medium-high heat. Add bacon and garlic; cook 4 minutes or until browned. Transfer to a bowl, leaving behind as much oil as possible. In batches, cook chicken pieces, turning occasionally, 5 minutes or until browned; add to bacon and onion mixture. Add brandy and red wine to pan, scraping up any browned bits from the bottom of the pan. Boil until reduced to about 1 tbsp (15 mL) of liquid.

2. In a piece of cheesecloth, tie together carrot, bay leaf and parsley. Add to pan along with 1 cup (250 mL) water, white wine, tomatoes, onions, roasted peppers and jalapenos. Bring to a boil; reduce heat to medium and simmer for 20 minutes or until reduced by half. Return the chicken, bacon and garlic to pan, reduce heat to low, cover and cook for 30 to 45 minutes or until chicken is cooked through. Discard carrot bundle.

3. If you desire a thicker stew, add *beurre manie* to sauce 1 tbsp (15 mL) at a time, stirring and simmering until sauce is thickened to your liking. Or, for a lower-fat thickener, mix 2 tbsp (25 mL) cornstarch with an equal amount of cold water and whisk into simmering stew. Serve chicken stew with GARLIC MASHED SPUDS.

Chicken with Cracked Wheat, Wild Mint and Pine Nuts

Cracked wheat is processed by prairie farmers in Saskatchewan. It makes a healthy, nutty base for this delicious chicken dish and is perfect for grain-based salads and pilafs. Pine nuts — found today in cuisines from Italy to the Orient — were also popular in Mexican and Native cooking. Pine nuts, or pinons, *grow on scrub pines in the Southwest, but these indigenous nuts are still a rare commodity in Western stores. Most of the pine nuts now sold here are grown in Asia.*

Serve this simple but flavorful dish with a salad of mixed greens and red tomatoes or radishes for a complete, colorful meal.

2 tbsp	olive oil	25 mL
2 to 3 lbs	boneless, skinless chicken thighs or 4 lbs (2 kg) chicken pieces, skinned	1 to 1.5 kg
1/2 tsp	salt	2 mL
1/4 tsp	freshly ground black pepper	1 mL
1	onion, chopped	1
2	cloves garlic, minced	2
1	jalapeno pepper, seeded and minced	1
3 cups	chicken stock	750 mL
1 1/2 cups	coarse cracked wheat *or* bulgar	375 mL
1/2 cup	toasted pine nuts	125 mL
2 tbsp	dark buckwheat honey or wildflower honey	25 mL
2 tbsp	chopped fresh mint (preferably wild)	25 mL
2 tsp	chopped fresh basil (optional)	10 mL

1. In a large Dutch oven, heat oil over medium-high heat. Sprinkle chicken with salt and pepper. In batches, cook chicken pieces 5 minutes, turning occasionally or until brown. Remove chicken from pan. Drain all but 1 tbsp (15 mL) of the accumulated fat. Reduce heat to medium. Cook onion, garlic and jalapeno pepper for 5 minutes or until onion is soft. Add stock. Bring to a boil, scraping browned bits off bottom of pan. Return chicken and accumulated juices to pan, reduce heat to medium-low, cover, and simmer for 20 minutes.

2. Remove chicken and set aside. Stir in wheat, pine nuts, honey and half of the chopped fresh mint. Distribute chicken pieces evenly over surface. Cover pan and continue to simmer 20 minutes longer or until chicken is cooked through and most of the liquid is absorbed. Remove pan from heat and let stand, covered, for 5 minutes. Fluff wheat mixture with a fork and transfer with chicken to a warm platter. Sprinkle with remaining chopped fresh mint and, if desired, basil.

Grilled Pheasant with Mustard Marinade

SERVES 4

My friend John Beckel is a hunter and comes back every season with wonderful wild pheasant from Southern Alberta. He grills the breasts on these simple but tasty kebabs to medium-rare perfection. If you can't find this tasty wild meat, substitute boneless, skinless chicken breasts; grill until chicken is cooked through.

PREHEAT BARBECUE

8 BAMBOO SKEWERS SOAKED IN WATER OR 8 METAL SKEWERS

8	small red potatoes (about 1 lb [500 g])	8
3 tbsp	honey	45 mL
2 tbsp	Dijon mustard	25 mL
1 tbsp	fresh lemon juice	15 mL
1/2 tsp	dried thyme leaves	2 mL
1/4 tsp	freshly ground black pepper	1 mL
1 lb	skinless boneless pheasant breasts, cut into 16 strips	500 g
8	large mushrooms, stems removed and halved	8
16	cherry tomatoes	16

1. Cut potatoes in half. Put in saucepan with cold water to cover. Bring to a boil, reduce heat and simmer 10 minutes or until almost tender. Drain and set aside.

2. In a bowl, whisk together honey, mustard, lemon juice, thyme and pepper. Add the pheasant and mushrooms and toss to coat in marinade. Marinate 30 minutes at room temperature.

3. Alternately thread the pheasant, mushroom halves, tomatoes and potatoes on skewers, discarding remaining marinade. Grill the kebabs on a covered grill for 8 minutes, turning occasionally, until pheasant is just cooked to medium rare.

Spicy Chicken and Beer Stew

This stew of skinless, boneless chicken thighs takes its inspiration from the spicy cuisine of Cajun country, where French Canadians settled in the mid-1700s after being drummed out of Acadia by the English. Spicy food is especially popular here in the West; with the north-south influence of Texas and other southern states comes barbecue, salsa and chili-spiked dishes like this. No doubt it would have been a favorite of the many African-American cowboys who road the early range in Texas after their release from slavery.

Serve this spicy dish with rice or cornbread.

1 tbsp	salt	15 mL
1 tbsp	garlic powder	15 mL
1 tbsp	cayenne pepper	15 mL
4 to 5 lbs	boneless skinless chicken thighs	2 to 2.2 kg
2/3 cup	all-purpose flour	150 mL
1/4 cup	canola oil	50 mL
1	large onion, chopped	1
2	stalks celery, chopped	2
3	cloves garlic, minced	3
1	green pepper, chopped	1
1	red pepper, chopped	1
1	jalapeno pepper, seeded and minced	1
2 cups	canned tomatoes, puréed until smooth in food processor	500 mL
1	bottle (12 oz [341 mL]) dark beer	1
1/2 cup	chicken stock	125 mL
1 tbsp	Worcestershire sauce	15 mL
2 tsp	dried marjoram	10 mL
2	bay leaves	2
	Pepper to taste	
	Cooked rice as accompaniment	

1. In a small bowl, stir together salt, garlic powder and cayenne pepper. Rub chicken all over with 1 tbsp (15 mL) of the spice mixture and let stand at room temperature for 30 minutes.

2. In a zippered plastic bag, combine flour with 1 tbsp (15 mL) of the spice mixture and shake chicken in spiced flour to coat. Reserve any excess spiced flour.

3. In a large Dutch oven, heat canola oil over medium-high heat. In batches, cook chicken 5 minutes or until browned. Set chicken aside.

One of the most famous cowboys to arrive in Alberta from Texas was John Ware, a black man who was born a slave in South Carolina. Ware became a cowboy after the Civil War, and signed on with Fred Stimson in 1882 to drive 3,000 head from Texas to the Bar U Ranch in southern Alberta.

Like other cowboys from the south, Ware brought his brand of American southern cooking to the area, still seen in the popularity of foods laced with chilies and southern-style barbecue.

John Ware acquired his own spread on the north fork of Sheep Creek in 1891. Many of his contemporaries considered him the finest Canadian horseman of his era.

4. Reduce heat to medium. Add reserved spiced flour to accumulated fat and oil in pan. Add an extra 1 tbsp (15 mL) of canola oil if necessary to create a smooth, creamy roux. Cook mixture, stirring constantly, for 10 minutes or until dark brown, the color of peanut butter. Stir in onion, celery, garlic, peppers and jalapenos; cook for 5 minutes. Stir in remaining spice mixture, tomatoes, beer, Worcestershire, marjoram and bay leaves. Return chicken to pan. Bring to a boil, reduce heat to low, cover and cook for 30 to 45 minutes or until chicken is cooked through, adding stock if the stew seems too thick. Season to taste with pepper. Serve over rice.

SERVES 4 TO 6

Grilled Spring Chicken with Rhubarb Sauce

You can double or triple the sauce used here, then bottle and preserve it. Place hot sauce into sterilized jars, seal and process in a boiling water bath for 20 minutes. This sauce is also nice with country pâtés and game.

Marinade

1 cup	orange juice	250 mL
1 tbsp	cider vinegar	15 mL
1 tbsp	honey	15 mL
1 tbsp	dry mustard	15 mL
1	chicken (about 4 lbs [2 kg]), cut up *or* 6 chicken breasts	1

Rhubarb Sauce

2 cups	diced rhubarb	500 mL
1/2 cup	fireweed honey or other wildflower honey	125 mL
2 tbsp	cider vinegar or balsamic vinegar	25 mL
2 tbsp	orange juice	25 mL
1 tsp	minced ginger root	5 mL
1	jalapeno pepper, seeded and minced	1
1	onion, chopped	1
2 tbsp	chopped fresh mint	25 mL

1. In a shallow glass baking dish, whisk together orange juice, cider vinegar, honey and mustard. Skin chicken pieces and add to marinade, turning to coat. Cover and refrigerate 4 hours or overnight in the refrigerator.

2. Rhubarb sauce: In a non-aluminum saucepan, stir together rhubarb, honey, vinegar, orange juice, ginger, jalapeno and onion. Bring to a boil, reduce heat to medium-low and simmer, uncovered, for 30 minutes or until the fruit breaks down and the sauce has a jam-like consistency. Cool to room temperature.

3. Preheat barbecue. Grill chicken over medium heat until cooked through, about 6 to 8 minutes per side. Serve topped with rhubarb sauce and garnished with mint.

Roast Duckling with Wild Berries

SERVES 4

Buy fresh ducks from Hutterite farmers at the markets during the summer months and from Chinatown butchers all year long. Or bag a wild duck during fall hunting season and enjoy this upscale preparation.

You can freeze your saskatoons or blueberries and make this elegant dish all winter long. Thaw berries before adding to sauce.

PREHEAT OVEN TO 500° F (260° C)
LARGE SHALLOW ROASTING PAN WITH RACK

| 2 | whole ducks (each about 4 lbs [2 kg]) | 2 |
| | Salt and pepper | |

Berry Sauce

2 tbsp	butter	25 mL
1/3 cup	granulated sugar	75 mL
1 1/2 cups	fresh orange juice	375 mL
1/2 cup	chicken stock	125 mL
1/2 cup	white wine vinegar	125 mL
1 cup	Saskatoon berries *or* blueberries	250 mL
1 tbsp	cognac or brandy	15 mL

1. Remove excess fat from cavity of ducks. Trim skin at neck end. Season ducks inside and out with salt and pepper. Prick skin with a fork, lifting skin away from meat. Place birds breast-side up on rack in roasting pan.

2. Roast for 30 minutes. Reduce heat to 350° F (180° C) and roast 60 to 75 minutes longer, basting occasionally with pan juices and removing some of fat if fat reaches level of rack, or until ducks are cooked through. Transfer to a platter and tent with foil to keep warm. Let stand 20 minutes before carving.

3. Meanwhile, make the sauce. In a heavy-bottomed saucepan, melt butter over medium heat. Stir in sugar; cook 4 minutes, stirring, or until sugar turns brown. Carefully add orange juice, stock and vinegar. Bring to a boil, stirring to dissolve caramelized sugar. Boil 5 minutes or until slightly thickened. Keep warm.

4. Just before serving, stir Saskatoon berries and cognac into the hot sauce and bring to a boil. To serve, carve legs and breasts into thin slices. Arrange meat on individual warm plates and top with sauce.

Turkey and Black Bean Burgers with Pickled Onion Rings

These tasty lean burgers are on the menu at the Rose Cafe and 4th Street Rose in Calgary. They make a nice change from the usual ground beef and, even better, are low in fat. The sweet pickled onions are great to have on hand for topping burgers or sandwiches in the summertime.

Turkey burgers can be frozen and reheat well.

If you want to cook your own beans, start with 1 cup (250 mL) dried black beans.

Use pickled onion slices on burgers, as here, or on salads of mixed bitter greens and sliced oranges, with cheese and pate, or to top sandwiches.

Pickled Onion Rings

1 lb	sweet onions (Walla Walla, Vidalia, Spanish or Bermuda)	500 g
6	peppercorns, lightly crushed	6
4	whole allspice berries	4
2	sprigs fresh thyme	2
1	bay leaf	1
2 tbsp	granulated sugar	25 mL
1/2 tsp	coarse salt	2 mL
1 cup	white wine vinegar	250 mL

Burgers

2 3/4 lbs	ground turkey	1.3 kg
2 1/2 cups	cooked black beans	625 mL
1 1/2 cups	dry bread crumbs	375 mL
3/4 cup	chopped fresh parsley	175 mL
4	eggs, lightly beaten	4
2	cloves garlic, minced	2
1	onion, minced	1
2 tbsp	Asian hot sauce (chili paste)	25 mL
1/2 tsp	salt	2 mL
Pinch	freshly ground black pepper	Pinch
Pinch	dried thyme leaves	Pinch
	Whole wheat buns, lettuce, tomato, cheese and barbecue sauce as accompaniments	

1. Make the pickled onion rings: Slice onions into thin rounds and put in a bowl. Pour boiling water to cover; drain. Put peppercorns, allspice, thyme, bay leaf, sugar and salt in a large jar. Fill jar with onion rings. Pour in 1 cup (250 mL) cold water and vinegar. Cover jar and shake slightly to dissolve sugar and salt, and to distribute the spices. Refrigerate for 2 weeks before using. (The onion rings will keep for weeks thereafter in the refrigerator.)

2. Make the burgers: Preheat barbecue. In a large bowl, combine turkey, black beans, bread crumbs, parsley, eggs, garlic, onion, hot sauce, salt, pepper and thyme. Mix well. Divide into 12 patties, 3/4-inch (15 mm) thick. Grill 10 to 12 minutes or until cooked through. Serve on whole wheat buns with lettuce, tomato, cheese and barbecue sauce.

eef is what we are famous for in this part of the world. No surprise there — it was beef cattle that opened up both the American and Canadian West. In fact, there were thousands of head of cattle on the Alberta prairie before there were more than a scattering of people. And after the first rush of American settlers to California in search of gold, Texans were soon populating the great southern plains with cattle. ⚘ Old-time cowboys survived on beef on the range and that's what you'll find on the table at branding parties and other cowboy celebrations today. From beefy chili to T-bone steak, prime rib or filet mignon, beef is always a popular choice. ⚘ Lamb is also making inroads in the local cooking community. Despite many old-timers' memories of strong-tasting mutton, lamb has been produced here since the earliest ranches were established. ⚘ At one time, sheep actually outnumbered cattle in the Wild West. The first domestic sheep came to the New World with the Spanish conquistadors and by the mid-1800s pioneers were bringing thousands of sheep to New Mexico, Arizona and southern California. ⚘ It was 1885 before cattle first outnumbered sheep in the U.S.. Cowboys hated sheep because they grazed the prairie grass down to its roots and destroyed the open range for cattle. Sheep were dubbed "hoofed locusts," leading to the legendary feuds between cattle and sheep producers — also providing fodder for Hollywood westerns — and leaving a bad taste for lamb in some parts of the West until fairly recently. ⚘ Today, locally produced lamb is in every western supermarket — a tender, mild alternative to the imported lamb coming from New Zealand and other countries. ⚘ Pork was also a prairie staple, with most farm families keeping at least a few pigs for their personal use. ⚘ Wild game — from rabbit to venison, elk and moose — was also an important part of early cowboy cuisine, and is gaining popularity again today as an especially lean, clean and healthy product. ⚘ Texas barbecue — slow smoking of beef or pork roasts over hot coals —

Beef, Lamb, Pork and Prairie Game

is also re-emerging in the West, with annual barbecue cook-offs from Calgary to Kansas City luring a new breed of competitive cowboy cook. ♞ This section contains recipes for the kind of barbecued beef you might see at a Stampede rodeo party or backyard barbecue, old-fashioned beef stews and ribs, plus gourmet ideas like a whole filet mignon with a four-peppercorn crust or an elegant venison steak in a berry and mushroom sauce. ♞ So chow down — red meat is back in style!

Flank Steak with Rye Whisky Marinade

SERVES 6

In the Wild West, whisky was a cowboy commodity that inspired many colorful handles, including "wild mare's milk", "tornado juice", "coffin varnish", "mountain dew" and "Brigham Young Cocktail" — of which it was said, "One sip and you're a confirmed polygamist."

Leftover grilled flank steak is great over mixed greens for steak salad or in STEAK AND POTATO SOUP (see recipe, page 33).

Be sure to avoid cooking flank steak to well done or it will be tough.

1/4 cup	rye whisky	50 mL
2 tbsp	soy sauce	25 mL
2 tbsp	minced fresh thyme	25 mL
2 tbsp	canola oil	25 mL
2 tsp	brown sugar	10 mL
1 tsp	chili powder	5 mL
1 tsp	coarsely crushed black peppercorns	5 mL
2	cloves garlic, minced	2
1	flank steak (about 1 1/2 lbs [750g])	1

1. In a bowl whisk together rye, soy sauce, thyme, oil, brown sugar, chili powder, peppercorns and garlic. Place in a zippered plastic bag with steak. Refrigerate overnight or up to 2 days, turning occasionally.

2. Remove steak from refrigerator at least 30 minutes before grilling. Grill over high heat for 4 to 5 minutes per side for medium-rare, brushing occasionally with marinade. Discard any leftover marinade.

3. Tent steak with foil and let stand for 5 minutes. Slice steak thinly across the grain on the diagonal to serve.

SERVES 6

Cowboy Steak

This dish is known as "chicken fried steak" in Texas, where they stir cream into the pan drippings to make a rich gravy. Texans, one Texas foodie remarked, need to have their chicken fried steak at least once a week and "only a rank degenerate would drive clear across Texas without stopping for a chicken fried steak." Likely left over from the days of long cattle drives, when steers killed on the trail were sinewy and tough, the steak benefits from being tenderized or pounded with flour and flavorings before cooking. Not a low-cal dish, but a traditional one on the prairies from Elko to Estevan.

3 lbs	round steak, cut 3/4 inch (2 cm) thick	1.5 kg
2 cups	all-purpose flour	500 mL
1 tsp	salt	5 mL
1 tsp	freshly ground black pepper	5 mL
1	egg	1
1/4 cup	milk *or* 10% cream	50 mL
	Canola oil for frying	
2 tbsp	all-purpose flour	25 mL
2 cups	milk *or* 10% cream	500 mL
	Salt and pepper to taste	

1. Cut steak into 6 pieces. In a shallow dish, combine 2 cups (500 mL) flour, salt and pepper; dip meat in flour mixture to coat. Pound steak with a meat mallet to about 1/4- to 1/2-inch (5 mm to 1 cm) thickness, to incorporate flour into meat and tenderize steaks; set aside. In a bowl, whisk together egg and 1/4 cup (50 mL) milk.

2. In a large cast iron frying pan, heat 1/4-inch (5 mm) canola oil over medium-high heat until sizzling. Dip meat into egg mixture, then into spiced flour to coat well; in two batches, cook steak 1 to 2 minutes or until browned on one side, then turn carefully and brown second side. Reduce heat to medium. Return all steak to pan. Add 3 tbsp (45 mL) water to the pan, cover and cook 8 minutes longer or until cooked through. Remove steak from pan and keep warm.

3. Stir 2 tbsp (25 mL) of flour into browned bits in pan; cook for 1 minute, stirring. Gradually add 2 cups (500 mL) milk or cream and cook, stirring, until cream gravy is thick and smooth. Season to taste with salt and pepper and serve over steaks.

Stampede Beef on a Bun

This is a perfect meal for the Stampede party or any big summer party crowd. It can be precooked the day before, then finished on the barbecue during the party. Set out some old washtubs filled with beer and ice, and serve some coleslaw and potato salad on the side. Yee-Ha!

LARGE SHALLOW ROASTING PAN
PREHEAT OVEN TO 300° F (150° C)

1	10-lb (5 kg) beef brisket	1
	Salt and freshly ground black pepper	
1	bottle (12 oz [341 mL]) dark beer	1
1 cup	ketchup	250 mL
1/2 cup	packed brown sugar	125 mL
1	large onion, minced	1
2 tbsp	Dijon mustard	25 mL
1 tbsp	dried basil	15 mL
1 tbsp	chili powder	15 mL
1 tbsp	Worcestershire sauce	15 mL
1 tsp	liquid smoke	5 mL
3	cloves garlic, crushed	3
	Crusty onion rolls	
	Beans, coleslaw, potato salad and/or baked potatoes as accompaniments	

1. Trim brisket and roll into an evenly shaped roast, tying at intervals. Sprinkle with salt and pepper. Place in roasting pan. In a bowl, whisk together beer, ketchup, brown sugar, onion, mustard, basil, chili powder, Worcestershire sauce, liquid smoke and garlic. Pour over meat. Cover pan tightly with foil. Roast for 4 hours. Remove roast and set aside to cool slightly, reserving sauce.

2. Preheat barbecue. Grill roast over medium-low heat 20 minutes, turning frequently, or until slightly charred and smoky. Meanwhile, bring cooking sauce to a boil and cook to thicken.

3. Thinly slice brisket. Add to simmering barbecue sauce. Serve on crusty onion rolls, with some of the barbecue sauce.

Leo's Roundup Beef Stew

Stews are synonymous with Western cooking — easy to cook over a campfire or to simmer on the back of a wood stove all day. Stews are rustic and heartwarming peasant fare throughout the world, and the best way to deal with tough, old or inferior cuts of meat.

Cowboy Leo Maynard makes this basic beef stew off the back of his chuckwagon with melt-in-your-mouth chunks of Alberta beef in a rich tomato sauce.

2 tbsp	canola oil	25 mL
2	onions, chopped	2
2	large green peppers, chopped	2
2	large red peppers, chopped	2
4 lbs	stewing beef, trimmed and cut into 1-inch (2.5 cm) cubes	2 kg
2	cans (each 28 oz [796 mL]) tomatoes	2
1 1/2 tsp	salt	7 mL
Pinch	garlic powder	Pinch
	Freshly ground black pepper	
	FLUFFY BAKING POWDER BISCUITS (see recipe, page 156) as accompaniment	

1. In a large Dutch oven, heat oil over medium-high heat; cook onions and peppers 10 minutes, stirring occasionally, or until softened and beginning to brown. Stir in beef, tomatoes, salt, garlic powder and black pepper to taste.

2. Bring to a boil. Reduce heat to low, cover and simmer for 3 hours, stirring occasionally, or until meat is tender. Serve with FLUFFY BAKING POWDER BISCUITS.

Barbecued Steak with Flavored Butters

There's really nothing easier that barbecuing or broiling a good cut of beef.

Choose a tender T-bone or Porterhouse steak. A Canada Grade AAA or USDA Prime grade steak has the most intramuscular fat and will grill up juiciest.

The best beef is well-aged — at least 14 to 21 days — and has a dark burgundy (not bright red) color. Aging breaks down some of the connective tissues in the meat, making it more tender. Supermarket meat usually sees minimal aging, so find a good butcher who knows how to handle beef.

While many people order lean tenderloin steaks in restaurants today, steak house chefs say the fattier rib eye is juicier and tastier.

Choose a steak that's at least 3/4-inch (1.5 cm) thick for barbecuing or broiling and make sure your grill is very hot — 475 to 500° F (250 to 260° C). Sear the steak one side, shifting it a quarter turn to get the classic cross-hatched grill marks on the meat, before turning it over to sear the second side. Douse any flare-ups with a squirt bottle of water. When the juice is starting to show on the top of the steak, it's done to perfection: medium-rare. Only a very thick steak needs to be shifted to a cooler spot on the grill and cooked longer than about 3 to 4 minutes per side. A 1-inch (2.5 cm) steak needs about 10 minutes of grill time — if the steak is 1 1/2 inches (3.5 cm) thick, grill 12 minutes. Bone-in steaks cook faster than boneless steaks.

Learn these "rules of thumb" for determining, by touch, how well your steak is done:

1. Press the triangle of flesh beneath your thumb when your hand is relaxed. It feels soft and spongy like a rare steak.
2. Touch your thumb and index finger together. Press the spot again and it will feel firmer, like a medium rare steak.
3. Touch your thumb and third finger together. Now your hand feels like a steak cooked to medium or medium well.
4. Touch your thumb to your fourth finger. The spot feels the same as a well-done steak, pretty bouncy and tough.
5. Now touch your thumb to your baby finger. The fleshy spot beneath your thumb is hard as a rock — and your steak is inedible!

Before grilling, rub steaks with olive oil, black pepper and garlic powder or seasoning salt. A little Worcestershire sauce also makes a nice rub for T-bones.

Handle your steaks with tongs, not a fork, which will puncture the seared crust and allow the meat to dry out.

A nice addition to any barbecued steak is a compound butter; a dab melting onto a steak just as it comes of the grill.

STEAK BUTTERS

Horseradish Butter

1/3 cup	softened butter	75 mL
2	green onions, minced *or* 1/2 cup (125 mL) chopped fresh chives	2
1	clove garlic, minced	1
3 tbsp	prepared horseradish	45 mL
1 tbsp	lemon juice	15 mL
1/2 tsp	freshly ground black pepper	2 mL

Tomato Peppercorn Butter

1/3 cup	softened butter	75 mL
1 tbsp	lemon juice	15 mL
1 tsp	peppercorn mixture (black, white, green and pink), roughly crushed	5 mL
2	oil-packed sun-dried tomatoes, drained and minced	2
1	clove garlic, minced	1

Blue Cheese Butter

1/3 cup	softened butter	75 mL
2 oz	blue cheese	50 g
1 tbsp	Dijon mustard	15 mL
1 tbsp	minced shallots	15 mL
1/2 tsp	freshly ground black pepper	2 mL

1. Put ingredients for the butter you choose in food processor and process until smooth; or, put in a bowl and combine well by hand.

2. Place butter in dollops, down the center of a piece of plastic wrap, and roll up to form a log, about 1 inch (2.5 cm) in diameter. Chill.

3. When steaks are ready, slice butter into coins and set 1 or 2 on each grilled steak just before serving.

SERVES 8 TO 10

Son-of-a-Bitch Stew

"A son-of-a-bitch may have no brains and no heart and still be a son-of-bitch. But if it don't have no guts, it's no son-of-a-bitch."

That's an old saying which refers to this eclectic stew — a specialty of every chuck-wagon cook, and a traditional dish for spring round-up, when calves were caught, branded and castrated. Traditionally made from the heart, liver, brains and entrails of a young calf, this stew testifies to the fact that cowboys on the range ate every last bit of the beef they butchered. In this version, however, we only use the name from the original; it includes traditional range staples like beef, beer and chilies, giving it as much creative kick as any authentic son-of-a-bitch, without all of the awful offal!

PREHEAT OVEN TO 325° F (160° C)

2	cloves garlic, minced	2
1 tsp	ground cumin	5 mL
1 tsp	salt	5 mL
1/2 tsp	pepper	2 mL
1/4 tsp	cinnamon	1 mL
1/4 cup	packed brown sugar	50 mL
5 lbs	boneless beef chuck steak, cut into 1 1/2-inch (3.5 cm) cubes	2 kg
2 tbsp	vegetable oil	25 mL
2	large onions, cut into wedges	2
1	green pepper, cut into chunks	1
1	bottle 12 oz [341 mL]) dark beer	1
2	tomatoes, diced *or* 3 tbsp (45 mL) tomato paste	2
1 tsp	dried chili flakes	5 mL
16	peeled baby carrots	16

1. In a small bowl, stir together garlic, cumin, salt, pepper, cinnamon and 1 tbsp (15 mL) of the brown sugar. Rub over beef and let stand for 1 hour at room temperature.

2. In a large ovenproof saucepan, heat oil over medium-high heat. In batches, cook meat, turning occasionally, for 5 minutes or until well-browned; transfer meat to a bowl. Add onions and green pepper to saucepan; cook 5 minutes or until softened. Return meat to saucepan. Stir in beer, tomato, chili flakes and remaining brown sugar. Cover, put in oven and bake for 2 hours.

3. Stir in carrots and potatoes, cover and cook 1 to 1 1/2 hours longer or until vegetables and beef are tender.

Spicy Barbecued Beef Ribs

PREHEAT OVEN TO 450° F (230° C)

4 lbs	beef short ribs *or* big beef side ribs	2 kg

Sauce

1 tbsp	canola oil	15 mL
1	onion, minced	1
2	cloves garlic, minced	2
1 1/2 cups	ketchup	375 mL
1/2 cup	chili sauce	125 mL
1/2 cup	strong brewed coffee	125 mL
1/4 cup	packed brown sugar	50 mL
1 tbsp	molasses	15 mL
1 tbsp	Worcestershire sauce	15 mL
1 tsp	liquid smoke	5 mL
1 tsp	hot pepper sauce	5 mL
1 tsp	freshly ground black pepper	5 mL
	Prepared horseradish, baked potatoes and beans as accompaniments	

" The Angus, Hereford and other shorthorn breeds are also the most prominent breeds in American cattle herds today, although the Texas longhorns dominated the American range between 1865 and 1885. Big and hardy, the longhorn were descended from the first cattle brought to the U.S. from Mexico and South America in the 1500s. They could withstand the harsh conditions on the American rangeland and the long drives to market, but soon became impractical both because of their dangerous horns (some more than 10 feet across), slower maturation and ultra-lean build.

The sauce used here is also good for marinating flank steak before barbecuing or for slathering on chicken burgers or other grilled meats.

1. Cut ribs into pieces. Put ribs in a large ovenproof saucepan and roast for 20 minutes.

2. Meanwhile, in a saucepan heat oil over medium heat. Add onion and garlic; cook for 3 minutes or until softened. Stir in ketchup, chili sauce, coffee, brown sugar, molasses, Worcestershire sauce, liquid smoke, hot sauce and pepper. Bring to a boil, reduce heat to medium-low and cook for 15 minutes.

3. Drain excess fat from ribs and pour the hot sauce over the ribs. Reduce oven temperature to 325° F (160° C) and bake, covered, for 1 to 1 1/2 hours or until meat is tender. Remove the cover and cook 15 minutes longer, basting them frequently with the sauce to glaze. Serve with lots of horseradish, beans and baked potatoes.

Beef Tenderloin with Four-Peppercorn Crust

This is one of those show-stopper beef dishes for special dinners. The tenderloin is expensive, but it's easy and so impressive! Serve with garlic mashed potatoes or stuffed baked potatoes, and sautéed wild mushrooms.

PREHEAT OVEN TO 425° F (220° C)
SHALLOW ROASTING PAN WITH A RACK

2 tbsp	black peppercorns	25 mL
2 tbsp	white peppercorns	25 mL
2 tbsp	green peppercorns	25 mL
2 tbsp	pink peppercorns	25 mL
1 tbsp	coarse salt	15 mL
1	whole beef tenderloin, about 3 to 4 lbs (1.5 to 2 kg), well-trimmed	1
3 tbsp	extra virgin olive oil	45 mL
	Mixed peppercorns and fresh thyme for garnish	

1. Combine the peppercorns in a bag. Crush coarsely with a mallet or rolling pin. Combine crushed peppercorns with salt.

2. Rinse beef and pat dry with paper towels, then rub with peppercorn-salt mixture, pressing the mixture into the meat. Let stand for 30 minutes at room temperature. (Recipe can be prepared to this point up to 2 days in advance; wrap meat tightly with plastic wrap and refrigerate. Bring to room temperature before proceeding with recipe.)

3. In a large nonstick frying pan, heat oil over high heat until smoking. Cook tenderloin, turning frequently, for 5 minutes or until well-browned on all sides. Place tenderloin on rack in roasting pan. Roast for 30 minutes for medium-rare.

4. Tent meat with foil and let stand 15 minutes. Slice crosswise into 1/2-inch (1 cm) slices and serve garnished with a sprinkle of mixed peppercorns and a sprig of thyme.

Texas-Style Barbecue

In Texas and points south, "barbecue" has a distinct definition — beef or sometimes pork, slow-smoked over indirect heat to tender perfection. While smoking or grilling meat over a grill has Spanish origins, the kind of barbecue they do south of the border has very little to do with our modern style of quickly searing and grilling foods.

In Texas barbecue joints, the big roasts are smoked for many hours, after being treated with spicy dry rubs and mopped with secret basting sauces. At Riscky's Texas Barbecue in Dallas, for instance, the famous sliced beef brisket is "rubbed with Riscky dust and smoked for 18 hours over a wood fire to perfection."

You can also buy a small electric or charcoal home smoker to approximate true slow barbecue.

1	beef brisket, about 4 lbs (2 kg)	1
1 tsp	black pepper	5 mL
1 tbsp	olive oil	15 mL
1 tbsp	dry mustard	15 mL
2 tsp	dried oregano	10 mL
1 tsp	ground sage	5 mL
1/2 tsp	cayenne pepper	2 mL
5	cloves garlic, minced	5
1	1-inch (2.5 cm) piece ginger root, minced	1
1/2 cup	ketchup	125 mL
1/4 cup	molasses	50 mL
1/4 cup	red wine vinegar	50 mL
1/4 cup	tomato paste	50 mL

1. In a shallow glass baking dish, rub brisket with pepper; set aside.

2. In a saucepan, heat oil over medium heat. Add mustard, oregano, sage, cayenne pepper, garlic and ginger; cook for 4 minutes, stirring constantly. Stir in 1 cup (250 mL) of water, ketchup, molasses, wine vinegar and tomato paste. Bring to a boil, reduce heat to medium-low and cook for 15 minutes. Cool. Pour marinade over roast, cover and refrigerate for 1 to 2 days, turning meat occasionally.

3. If using a gas barbecue, light one burner only and place meat on unlit side with drip pan below grill and under roast; lower lid. In a conventional smoker, cook with beer or wine in the drip pan. For a covered charcoal barbecue, heat coals, then move them around the outside edges of grill with drip pan and meat in the middle. Maintain an even heat of 200° F (100° C), adding preheated coals throughout smoking period.

4. Cook 5 to 6 hours, or until meat thermometer reads 150° F (65° C), turning occasionally and basting meat with marinade as it cooks. Add more coals as necessary to smoker or charcoal grill, and toss in some damp wood chips occasionally for smoke. Let stand 10 minutes before slicing. Serve with homemade or commercial barbecue sauce.

Old-Fashioned Meat Loaf with Tomato Gravy

PREHEAT OVEN TO 375° F (190° C)
9- BY 5-INCH (2 L) LOAF PAN

*S*cratch a prairie cook — or just about anyone, for that matter — and you'll probably find a love of meatloaf. Used as leftovers the next day, this loaf makes great sandwiches with pickled onions, chutney and lettuce.

Mince the vegetables in a food processor for a very fine result.

1 tbsp	butter	15 mL
2	cloves garlic, minced	2
1	large onion, minced	1
1	stalk celery, minced	1
Half	red bell pepper, minced	Half
2 lbs	lean ground beef	1 kg
8 oz	ground pork *or* minced bacon	250 g
1/2 cup	tomato sauce *or* barbecue sauce	125 mL
2	large eggs, beaten	2
1/2 tsp	ground cumin	2 mL
1 tsp	salt	5 mL
1/2 tsp	black pepper	2 mL
Pinch	cayenne pepper	Pinch
3/4 cup	dry bread crumbs	175 mL

Tomato Gravy

3 tbsp	olive oil	45 mL
3 tbsp	all purpose flour	45 mL
1 cup	beef stock	250 mL
1/4 cup	white wine *or* sherry	50 mL
1/4 cup	minced oil-packed sun-dried tomatoes	50 mL
3 tbsp	tomato paste	45 mL
2 tbsp	minced garlic	25 mL
1 tbsp	chopped fresh basil	15 mL
1 cup	milk	250 mL
	Salt and pepper to taste	

1. In a saucepan, melt butter over medium-high heat. Add garlic, onion, celery and red pepper; cook 10 minutes or until vegetables are tender and liquid has been absorbed. Cool.

2. In a large bowl and using your hands, mix beef and pork. Mix in tomato sauce, eggs, cumin, salt, pepper and cayenne. Add the cooled vegetables and bread crumbs, kneading with your hands to combine well. Pack mixture into loaf pan. Bake for 1 hour and 15 minutes or until firm and well-browned. Let loaf rest 20 minutes before slicing.

3. Gravy: In a saucepan, heat oil over medium heat. Stir in flour; cook, stirring, for 1 minute. Whisk in the beef stock, wine, sun-dried tomatoes, tomato paste, garlic and basil. Bring to a boil, stirring. Cook until smooth and thickened. Stir in milk and heat through. Season to taste with salt and pepper.

4. Drain excess fat from meatloaf. Slice thickly. Serve with tomato gravy.

SERVES 4

Roasted Rack of Lamb with Onion Jam

This recipe comes from the talented culinary students and their instructors at the Southern Alberta Institute of Technology. Make extra onion jam and use it to top savory sandwiches or pizzas, or as an appetizer with French bread.

To "french" lamb racks, remove spine bone and trim all of the meat, fat and sinew away from the ends of the rib bones.

2	racks Alberta lamb (7 ribs each), frenched	2
1 tbsp	olive oil	15 mL

Marinade

1 cup	coarse-grained Dijon mustard	250 mL
1	sprig fresh rosemary, leaves only	1
8	black peppercorns, crushed	8
2	cloves garlic, crushed	2

Onion jam

2 tbsp	butter	25 mL
8 oz	onions or shallots, peeled and sliced	250 g
1/4 cup	white wine	50 mL
2 tbsp	granulated sugar	25 mL

Sauce

2 tbsp	red wine	25 mL
2 cups	lamb stock *or* beef stock	500 mL
1	clove garlic, crushed	1
1/2 tsp	chopped fresh rosemary	2 mL
	Salt and pepper to taste	
	Steamed vegetables and roasted potatoes as accompaniments	

1. Marinade: In a food processor, combine mustard, rosemary, peppercorns and garlic; purée until smooth. With a brush, generously coat the entire racks of lamb with the marinade. Cover and refrigerate overnight.

2. Onion jam: In a heavy saucepan, melt butter over medium heat. Stir in onions, sugar and white wine. Reduce heat to medium-low and cook, uncovered and stirring occasionally, 30 minutes or until onions are soft and caramelized. Set aside. (Jam can be made in advance and reheated before serving.)

3. Bring lamb to room temperature. Preheat oven to 375° F (190° C). In an ovenproof frying pan, heat olive oil over medium-high heat. One at a time, cook lamb racks, turning occasionally, for 4 minutes or until well browned. Return both racks to pan; stand them up, interlocking the rib bones. Roast for 30 minutes or until a meat thermometer reads 130° F (65° C) for medium-rare.

4. Remove lamb from pan, tent with foil and keep warm. Discard the fat in the pan and stir the red wine into the pan drippings. Bring to a boil, scraping browned bits off bottom of pan. Add the stock, garlic and rosemary. Boil until reduced to about 3/4 cup (175 mL). Strain sauce and season to taste with salt and pepper.

5. Carve the lamb with a sharp knife, cutting between the ribs. Arrange lamb over a mound of warm onion jam on each of four plates, with rib bones pointing up at the center of the plate. Drizzle with sauce and serve with steamed vegetables and roasted potatoes.

Lamb and Cornmeal Shepherd's Pie

The first domestic sheep came to the New World with the Spanish conquistadors. By the mid-1800s, pioneers were bringing thousands of sheep to New Mexico, Arizona and southern California.

In 1884, the British American Ranche at Cochrane received the first large sheep herd in Alberta — 8,000 Merino sheep driven across the prairie in a seething wooly mass from Montana. Later the Mormons around Raymond and Magrath took over the role of raising sheep. In 1921, most of the province's 432,000 sheep were in the hands of Mormon ranchers.

PREHEAT OVEN TO 500° C (260° C)
BAKING SHEET
13- BY 9-INCH (3 L) BAKING DISH

Topping

4 cups	milk	1 L
1 1/4 cups	cornmeal	300 mL
6	extra large eggs	6
1 cup	grated Parmesan cheese	250 mL

Roasted Tomato Sauce

1 1/2 lbs	plum tomatoes, halved, seeded and cored	750 g
1	jalapeno pepper, halved, stemmed and seeded	1
1	onion, cut into eighths	1
2	cloves garlic, peeled	2
1 tbsp	olive oil	15 mL

Meat Mixture

1 1/2 lbs	ground lamb	750 g
2 tbsp	chopped ginger root	25 mL
1	onion, minced	1
2	cloves garlic, minced	2
3 tbsp	soy sauce	45 mL
	Salt and freshly ground pepper	

1. Topping: In a deep, heavy saucepan, bring milk to a boil over medium heat. Add cornmeal in a slow, steady stream, whisking constantly. Reduce heat to low and continue to cook, stirring frequently, for 5 minutes or until thick and smooth. Remove from heat. Cool slightly. Stir in eggs, one at a time, beating well after each addition. Stir in cheese. Set aside.

2. Roasted tomato sauce: In a bowl stir together tomatoes, jalapeno, onion, garlic and olive oil. Spread out on baking sheet. Bake 30 minutes, stirring occasionally, or until vegetables are brown and begin to char. Transfer to a food processor; purée and set aside. Reduce oven temperature to 325° F (160° C).

3. In a large frying pan set over medium heat, cook ground lamb, stirring to break meat up, 8 minutes or until no longer pink. Drain any accumulated fat. Add the ginger, onion and garlic; cook 5 minutes longer or until onion is tender. Stir in soy sauce and roasted tomato sauce. Season to taste with salt and pepper.

4. Spread meat mixture over bottom of baking dish. Smooth cornmeal topping over meat. Bake for 1 hour or until topping is golden.

Pork and Black Bean Stew with Sweet Potatoes

This is a gorgeous stew — tender pieces of boneless pork, highlighted by shiny black beans and cubes of deep orange sweet potatoes. A sprinkling of chopped cilantro just before serving adds real Western flavor and even more bright color to the mix. I like this healthy combination served with a mound of creamy mashed potatoes or cornbread.

To save time, use canned black beans, rinsed and drained.

PREHEAT OVEN TO 350° F (180° C)
12-CUP (3 L) CASSEROLE DISH WITH LID

2 tbsp	olive oil	25 mL
4 lbs	boneless pork shoulder, cut into 1-inch (2.5 cm) cubes	2 kg
2 tbsp	all-purpose flour	25 mL
2	sweet potatoes (about 1 lb [500 g]), peeled and cubed	2
1 1/2 cups	chicken stock	375 mL
1 1/2 cups	chopped onions	375 mL
1 cup	dry white wine	250 mL
1/2 cup	chopped fresh parsley	125 mL
1/4 cup	red wine vinegar	50 mL
6	cloves garlic, minced	6
1 tbsp	ground cumin	15 mL
2 cups	cooked black beans	500 mL
1 tsp	ground cumin	5 mL
1/2 tsp	freshly ground black pepper	2 mL
1/2 cup	chopped cilantro	125 mL

1. In a large frying pan, heat oil over medium-high heat. In batches, cook pork, turning occasionally, for 5 minutes or until browned. Transfer pork to casserole dish as it is browned.

2. Sprinkle flour over the pork and toss. Add the sweet potatoes, chicken stock, onions, wine, parsley, vinegar, half of the garlic and 1 tbsp (15 mL) of cumin; mix well. Cover and bake for 1 hour.

3. Stir in beans, 1 tsp (5 mL) cumin, pepper and remaining garlic. Bake, uncovered, for 15 minutes or until slightly thickened. Just before serving, stir in the cilantro.

Pork Wraps with Green Tomatoes and Ancho Chilies

Fiery chili peppers have always been part of Mexican cuisine and were popular with early Mexican and Black cowboys in the southwest. But it was actually the Spanish that first introduced chili peppers to southwestern native tribes in the 16th century.

The mildest chilies are long, New Mexico or Anaheim chilies, the long chilies dried in ropes or ristras in the south.

Poblanos are also a mild chili, eaten green or dried to become pasillas.

Jalapeno peppers may be green or red, ranging from mildly hot to seriously searing. Dried and smoked jalapeno peppers are called chipotles; they are sold dry or canned.

PREHEAT OVEN TO 350° F (180° C)

2 tbsp	olive oil	25 mL
2 lbs	boneless pork shoulder, cut into 1-inch (2.5 cm) cubes	1 kg
6	cloves garlic, peeled	6
1	large onion, chopped	1
1/2 tsp	salt	2 mL
1 lb	tomatillos or green tomatoes, chopped *or* 1 can (28 oz [796 mL] tomatillos, drained)	500 g
1 lb	ripe tomatoes, chopped	500 g
1 cup	dark beer	250 mL
1 cup	orange juice	250 mL
1	jalapeno pepper, seeded and chopped	1
2	dried ancho or pasilla chilies, seeded and crumbled	2
1 tsp	ground cumin	5 mL
1 cup	chopped cilantro	250 mL
8 oz	fresh spinach, chopped	250 g
12	large flour tortillas	12
	Chopped fresh tomatoes and sour cream as toppings	

1. In a large ovenproof saucepan, heat oil over medium-high heat. In batches, cook pork, turning occasionally, 5 minutes or until browned. Return all meat to pan. Stir in garlic, onions and salt; cook 10 minutes or until onions begin to brown. Stir in tomatillos, tomatoes, beer, orange juice, jalapeno, crumbled chilies and cumin.

2. Cover and bake uncovered for 1 1/4 hours or until pork is tender. Stir in chopped cilantro and spinach; cook, stirring, until greens are just wilted.

3. Serve with large flour tortillas for wrapping and let your guests create their own wraps. Place about 3/4 cup (175 mL) of the pork and spinach mixture into a tortilla, top with some sour cream and chopped fresh tomatoes. Fold the bottom third up over the filling, then roll to enclose.

Grilled Baby Back Ribs with Beer Barbecue Sauce

SERVES 4

This sauce, developed for a cooking class by Calgary's Lorna Hurst, also works well for pork tenderloin and chicken. It will keep for up to 1 month in the refrigerator or freeze in zippered plastic bags.

Sauce

2 tbsp	canola oil	25 mL
6	cloves garlic, minced	6
3	jalapeno peppers, seeded and minced	3
1	large onion, minced	1
1 tbsp	minced ginger root	15 mL
3/4 cup	white wine vinegar	175 mL
1	bottle (12 oz [341 mL]) dark ale	1
2 cups	tomato sauce	500 mL
1 cup	packed brown sugar *or* maple syrup	250 mL
1/3 cup	molasses	75 mL
1/3 cup	dark soy sauce	75 mL
	Salt and hot sauce to taste	
4 lbs	racks baby back ribs	2 kg

1. In a saucepan, heat oil over medium-high heat. Add garlic, jalapenos, onion and ginger; cook for 4 minutes or until starting to brown. Stir in vinegar, scraping up browned bits. Stir in beer. Bring to a boil; cook until reduced by one third. Add tomato sauce, brown sugar, molasses and soy sauce. Bring to a boil. Reduce heat to low and simmer, covered, for 1 hour. Season to taste with salt and hot sauce. Cool and refrigerate.

2. In a large saucepan add water to cover to ribs. Bring to a boil. Reduce heat to medium and simmer, uncovered, for 30 minutes. Drain and cool. In a large shallow baking dish, combine cooled ribs and 2 cups (500 mL) barbecue sauce. Cover and refrigerate overnight.

3. Preheat barbecue. Grill ribs over medium heat for 10 minutes, turning and brushing occasionally with reserved marinade, until crisp and starting to blacken. Serve with extra barbecue sauce on the side.

STAMPEDE BEEF ON A BUN (PAGE 80) ➤

OVERLEAF: BARBECUED STEAK WITH FLAVORED BUTTERS (PAGE 82)

SERVES 4

Grilled Venison Steaks in Wild Berry, Sage and Mushroom Sauce

If fresh wild mushrooms are not available, use dried mushrooms — rehydrate and chop before using in recipe.

Saskatoon berries are the quintessential prairie berry. Also known as the serviceberry, these bush-grown berries resemble a blueberry but with a distinctive sweet flavor and drier texture.

Ripe in July, wild saskatoons can still be found growing in the coulees and along river banks across the western prairies, but you can also plant your own domestic saskatoon berry bushes and harvest crops in your own backyard

4	boneless venison medallions (each about 5 oz [200 g]), from tenderloin *or* 4 small beef tenderloin filets	4
Marinade		
1/4 cup	olive oil	50 mL
2 tbsp	minced shallots	25 mL
2 tsp	minced fresh sage	10 mL
1/2 tsp	black pepper	2 mL
Sauce		
1 tbsp	olive oil	15 mL
1/2 cup	chopped shallots	125 mL
1 cup	Cabernet Sauvignon or Pinot Noir	250 mL
1 cup	beef stock	250 mL
1/2 cup	chopped wild mushrooms	125 mL
1 cup	fresh wild berries (blueberries, saskatoons *or* cranberries)	250 mL
1 tbsp	chopped fresh sage	15 mL
1 to 2 tbsp	wild honey	15 to 25 mL
	Salt and freshly ground pepper to taste	
	Sprigs fresh sage as garnish	
	Wild rice pilaf *or* garlic mashed potatoes as accompaniment	

1. Marinade: In a shallow glass baking dish, whisk together olive oil, shallots, sage and black pepper. Add venison, turning to coat. Cover and refrigerate overnight.

2. Sauce: In a frying pan, heat oil over medium-high heat. Cook shallots 5 minutes or until golden. Stir in 1 cup (250 mL) water, wine, stock, and mushrooms. Bring to a boil. Add berries and sage, reduce heat to medium and simmer for 15 minutes or until sauce will coat a spoon. Season to taste with honey, salt and pepper. Keep warm.

3. Grill venison medallions to rare or medium-rare, about 5 minutes per side. Place on individual warm plates and top with sauce. Garnish with sprigs of fresh sage and serve with wild rice pilaf or garlic mashed potatoes.

◄ ROASTED RACK OF LAMB WITH ONION JAM (PAGE 90)

Buffalo and Root Vegetable Stew

SERVES 6 TO 8

PREHEAT OVEN TO 300° F (150° C)
12-CUP (3 L) CASSEROLE DISH WITH LID

2 cups	julienned carrots	500 mL
1 cup	julienned parsnips	250 mL
1 lb	pearl onions, peeled	500 g
2 tbsp	bacon fat *or* canola oil	25 mL
1/4 cup	butter	50 mL
3 lbs	boneless buffalo shoulder *or* stewing beef, cut into 2-inch (5 cm) cubes	1.5 kg
3 tbsp	all-purpose flour	45 mL
1 1/2 tsp	chopped fresh basil	7 mL
1 tsp	salt	5 mL
1/2 tsp	freshly ground black pepper	2 mL
1	clove garlic, minced	1
1 cup	red wine	250 mL
Pinch	granulated sugar	Pinch
3/4 cup	Madeira *or* port	175 mL
1/4 cup	brandy *or* cognac	50 mL
	Cooked wide noodles, mashed potatoes, biscuits *or* Native flatbread as accompaniment	

1. In a large saucepan, combine carrots, parsnips and pearl onions. Add water to cover. Bring to a boil; cook 1 to 2 minutes or until tender-crisp. Drain, reserving cooking liquid. Set vegetables and liquid aside.

2. In a heavy frying pan, melt 2 tbsp (25 mL) of the butter with bacon fat over medium-high heat. In batches, cook meat, turning, 3 minutes or until browned. (Transfer meat to casserole dish as it is browned.) Reduce heat to medium. Stir flour, basil, salt, pepper and garlic into fat in pan, adding up to 1 tbsp (15 mL) additional canola oil as necessary to make a smooth paste. Cook, stirring, for 1 minute or until browned.

When the Europeans arrived in the Old West, they traded for buffalo hides; so great was the demand for buffalo robes that it led to the near extinction of the animals between 1860 and 1878. The plains were littered with the whitening bones of these massive animals, creating a short-lived secondary industry between 1884 and 1897. Buffalo bones and skulls were collected by the thousands, and piled at railway sidings where they were shipped to American fertilizer plants. The bones brought $5.50 to $8.50 a ton, and by 1897 the prairies were virtually picked clean, with more than 22,000 tons of buffalo bones collected and sent south.

3. Measure 2 cups (500 mL) of reserved vegetable cooking liquid, adding water if necessary; gradually whisk liquid and wine into flour. Cook, stirring, until smooth and thickened. Pour over meat in casserole, cover and cook for 3 hours or until meat is almost tender.

4. In a large frying pan, melt remaining 2 tbsp (25 mL) butter over medium-high heat. Stir in sugar. Cook drained onions, carrots and parsnips 8 minutes or until lightly browned and caramelized. Add vegetables to the stew along with the Madeira. Bake, uncovered, for 30 minutes longer or until meat and vegetables are tender.

5. Just before serving, stir in brandy. Thin with extra vegetable cooking liquid or water, if desired. Serve with mashed potatoes, wide noodles, biscuits or a traditional Native flatbread, such as INDIAN FRYBREAD (see recipe, page 126).

After mountain skiing and hiking, fly-fishing is now becoming the trendiest sport among locals and visitors to the West. ⚞ I'm no fisherman, but I will never forget catching a mess of perch off the dock with my dad (on a hook baited with miniature marshmallows) or the day I pulled a big lake trout out of a tiny lake in the Sweetgrass Hills on the Montana border. ⚞ Fly fishing for trout has become more than an idle pastime for those looking for a lovely meal. All kinds of men and women are heading out with their fishing gear to western waterways today. And with high-end tackle stores offering everything from graphite rods to belly boats, as well as outfitters luring tourists with float trips down the mighty Madison and Bow rivers, there is a definite industry that's grown up around the trout in the streams. ⚞ Rainbow trout, lake trout, brown trout — they're all easy to catch with the right tackle, as are fish like Rocky Mountain whitefish, perch and pike. Further north, western waters offer arctic char, pickerel and BIG lake trout. ⚞ While you'll have to head over the border into BC for salmon, this fish is also popular on the prairies since it is widely available (unlike the early years, when it only came in cans). ⚞ Nothing beats a shore lunch of fresh trout, split and barbecued on a green twig over an open fire or filleted, dipped in seasoned flour and fried in butter. But back at the ranch you can try these recipes for whole trout, grilled with black beans and corn, old-fashioned fillets, battered and fried, or poached salmon glazed with red wine. It's the kind of fish we enjoy here in the land-locked West.

Fish

Grilled Whole Trout with Black Bean and Corn Salsa

Trout is a trophy fish in the cold mountain streams, rivers and lakes of the Rocky Mountains and foothills that run from Alberta through Montana and Colorado to New Mexico. Cowboys have always loved to spend their spare time fishing — and today, rivers such as the Bow (in Alberta) and the Madison (in Montana) are havens for a new generation of fly fishers.

Salsa

2 cups	corn (preferably from fresh corn on the cob that's been grilled in the husk and removed from the cob) *or* thawed frozen kernels	500 mL
2 cups	cooked black beans *or* 1 can (19 oz [540 mL])	500 mL
1 tbsp	jalapeno pepper, seeded and minced (about 1 pepper)	15 mL
1	small tomato, seeded and diced	1
2 tbsp	olive oil	25 mL
	Juice of 1 lime	
2 tbsp	chopped cilantro	25 mL
4	small trout (about 1 lb [500 g] each), cleaned	4
	Salt and pepper to taste	

1. In a large bowl, combine corn, black beans, jalapeno pepper, sugar, cumin, black beans, vinegar, tomato, olive oil, lime juice and cilantro.
2. Wipe a grill basket, large enough to hold the fish in a single layer, with oil. Season fish inside and out with salt and pepper.
3. Barbecue fish over medium high heat, turning several times, about 10 to 12 minutes in total or until fish flakes easily. Serve each person a whole fish, with 1/2 cup (125 mL) of salsa on the side, passing extras.

Fish Fillets with Chili Pepper Pesto

ere is an easy fish dish, full of the savory spices and feisty flavors of the West. Use boneless, skinless white fish fillets for this speedy but impressively flavored feast.

Ancho or poblano peppers are about 4 inches (10 cm) long, cone-shaped, with a mild, almost raisin-like flavor. You can substitute the slightly hotter pasillas in this dish; they're also mild but are longer and narrower. You can find both dried anchos and pasillas in packages in the produce section of most major supermarkets.

LARGE RIMMED BAKING SHEET, OILED
PREHEAT OVEN TO 450° F (220° C)

3	dried ancho or pasilla chilies	3
2 tbsp	canola oil	25 mL
1	onion, chopped	1
1/4 cup	toasted pine nuts	50 mL
3	cloves garlic	3
1	large red bell pepper, chopped	1
2 tbsp	orange juice	25 mL
1 tsp	lemon juice	5 mL
1/2 tsp	salt	2 mL
1 cup	cilantro leaves	250 mL
2 lbs	fish fillets (snapper, halibut, perch, sole, etc.)	1 kg
	Lime wedges, chopped cilantro and Mexican-style rice as accompaniments	

1. Soak dried chilies in hot water for 30 minutes or until softened. Drain; discard seeds and stems. Set aside.

2. In a frying pan, heat oil over medium-high heat; cook onion 8 minutes or until golden. Place in food processor with chilies, pine nuts, garlic, red pepper, orange juice, lemon juice and salt. Process to form a paste. Add cilantro to food processor; pulse until herbs are coarsely chopped.

3. Place fish fillets in a single layer on baking sheet. Spread pesto over filets, smoothing it over the entire surface of the fish. Set aside for 10 minutes at room temperature to marinate.

4. Bake the fish for 10 minutes per 1 inch (2.5 cm) thickness of fish, or until fish just begins to flake. Serve sprinkled with cilantro, with lime wedges and rice on the side.

Pan-Fried Trout with Sage and Almond Crust

1/2 cup	sliced almonds	125 mL
1/4 cup	whole wheat flour	50 mL
2 tbsp	ground sage	25 mL
1 tsp	salt	5 mL
1/2 tsp	freshly ground black pepper	2 mL
Pinch	cayenne pepper	Pinch
4	trout (each about 12 oz [375 g]), scaled and gutted, head and tail on	4
3 tbsp	olive oil	45 mL
1 tbsp	butter	15 mL
	Lemon wedges for garnish	
	Cooked wild rice and almonds as accompaniments	

1. In a food processor combine almonds, flour, sage, salt, black pepper and cayenne pepper; process until fine. Place in a zippered plastic bag. One at a time, place whole trout in the bag of seasoned flour and shake to coat.

2. Divide butter and oil between two cast iron or heavy nonstick frying pans. Melt over medium-high heat. Cook trout for about 10 minutes or until cooked through and golden on both sides, reducing heat to medium if skin gets too brown. Squeeze some lemon juice over top just before serving. Serve with wild rice and almonds.

Freshly caught and pan-fried over a fire, there is nothing finer than a pretty rainbow or brown trout.

Wrote Brillat-Savarin in Physiology of Taste *in 1838: "Do not forget, however, when you have any of those trout weighing scarcely more than a quarter of a pound caught in running brooks that murmur far from the capital — do not forget, I say, to fry them in the very finest olive oil you have. This simple dish, properly sprinkled and served up with slices of lemon is worth of being offered to a cardinal."*

Prepare the coating at home and take it along to the campsite — or wherever you plan to catch a few trout.

Beer-Battered Fish Fillets

Although deep-fried food is technically a no-no in these health-conscious times, you wouldn't know it to count the number of fish-and-chips shops still thriving in the West. Whether it's the lingering influence of early British settlers or our penchant for fast food, our love of old-fashioned fish and chips looks like it's around to stay. Using a local micro-brewed beer in the batter makes it even better.

1 cup	all-purpose flour	250 mL
1/2 cup	whole wheat flour	125 mL
1 tsp	paprika	5 mL
1/2 tsp	salt	2 mL
1	bottle (12 oz [341 mL]) pale ale	1
1	egg	1
1 tbsp	canola oil	15 mL
3 lbs	fish fillets (such as cod, trout, snapper)	1.5 kg
1/2 cup	all-purpose flour, for coating	125 mL
	Canola oil for frying	
	Lemon wedges *or* tartar sauce for garnish	

1. In a large bowl, combine 1 cup (250 mL) all-purpose flour, whole wheat flour, paprika and salt. Beat in beer, egg and oil until smooth. Let batter stand for 2 hours.

2. In a wok or heavy deep saucepan, heat about 2 inches (5 cm) of oil to 350° F (180° C). A few pieces at a time, coat fillets in remaining flour by rolling them in flour on a plate or gently shaking them with flour in a paper bag. Dip floured fish in batter to coat, shake off excess, and set in hot oil to fry. Fry about 6 minutes, turning half way, or until golden brown on both sides. Drain on paper towels and serve hot, garnished with lemon wedges or tartar sauce.

Grilled Trout in Foil Packets with Cracked Wheat and Vegetables

Bulgar is a Middle Eastern staple, the basis of tabouli salads and other meatless dishes. It is also good for you — about 12% protein, 2% fat, 2.2% fibre and 70% carbohydrates, with 30 to 35% more protein by weight than rice, corn or barley. Because of the way it is processed, bulgar loses little of its natural food value.

To make bulgar, whole kernels of wheat are boiled, then dried and broken into bits. Cracked wheat is a different product — it is simply made from coarsely ground raw wheat, with the wheat germ removed to improve shelf life. Cracked wheat needs to be cooked, while bulgar only needs soaking to rehydrate.

HEAVY FOIL
PREHEAT BARBECUE

4	trout fillets (about 6 to 8 oz [200 to 250 g] each)	4
1/2 tsp	salt	2 mL
1/8 tsp	black pepper	0.5 mL
3/4 cup	bulgar *or* coarse cracked wheat	175 mL
1/2 cup	chopped seeded tomatoes	125 mL
1/2 cup	shredded carrots	125 mL
1/3 cup	chopped green peppers	75 mL
4	green onions, chopped	4
1/4 cup	chopped fresh parsley	50 mL
1/4 cup	white wine *or* water	50 mL
1/4 cup	olive oil	50 mL
1 tsp	chopped fresh rosemary	5 mL
1/4 tsp	salt	1 mL
8	lemon slices	8

1. Tear heavy foil into four 12-inch (30 cm) squares.
2. Cut each fillet in half. Sprinkle with 1/2 tsp (2 mL) salt and pepper.
3. In a bowl, stir together bulgar, tomatoes, carrots, green peppers, onions, parsley, water, oil, rosemary and 1/4 tsp (1 mL) salt. Place one-quarter of the bulgar mixture on each foil square. Top each with two pieces of fish and 2 lemon slices. Tightly seal packages.
4. Grill over medium heat for 15 minutes, turning once during cooking. Alternately, place the packets on a baking sheet and bake at 400° F (200° C) for 15 to 20 minutes or until fish flakes easily.

SERVES 4

Baked Whole Trout, Stuffed with Wild Rice and Wrapped in Sorrel Leaves

orrel can be hard to find but this tart-tasting green grows wild in the woods and is easily grown in city gardens. Wood sorrel has three leaves and resembles a shamrock. Field sorrel is considered a weed, and its leaves look more like a dandelion, but both are a tasty green with a sharp, lemony flavor. Try it in soups, salads or sandwiches. If you are unable to find fresh sorrel, wrap these stuffed trout in fresh spinach leaves before baking.

PREHEAT OVEN TO 450° F (230° C)

4	small trout (about 1 lb [500 g] each)	4
	Salt and pepper to taste	

Stuffing

1 tbsp	olive oil	15 mL
1	small onion, minced	1
1	garlic clove, minced	1
4 oz	chopped wild mushrooms	250 g
1/2 cup	chicken stock	125 mL
1/4 cup	dried cranberries	50 mL
1 cup	cooked wild rice	250 mL
	Salt and pepper to taste	
1 tbsp	minced fresh dill	15 mL
	Fresh sorrel leaves (or spinach leaves), washed and spun dry	
	Fresh lemon slices as garnish	

1. Salt and pepper fish cavities. Set aside.

2. In a saucepan heat oil over medium heat. Add onion and garlic; cook 5 minutes or until softened. Add mushrooms and cook until tender. Stir in stock and cranberries; simmer 2 minutes. Add wild rice and dill; stir until well mixed. Season to taste with salt and pepper.

3. Stuff rice-mushroom mixture into fish cavities and close with toothpicks or skewers.

4. Wrap fish in moist sorrel leaves or spinach and set on an oiled rack in a shallow roasting pan. Bake in preheated oven for 15 to 20 minutes, or until fish flakes from bones. Garnish with thin slices of fresh lemon (or, if using spinach, top wrapped fish with lemon slices before baking).

Barbecued Salmon with Whisky Marinade

Whisky makes a classic Western addition to this dish — as it does to many sauces and marinades. Use it whenever you'd otherwise deglaze with cognac or reach for rum to flambée fruit.

1/2 cup	rye whisky	125 mL
1/4 cup	olive oil	50 mL
2 tbsp	soy sauce	25mL
2 tbsp	brown sugar	25 mL
4	crushed garlic cloves	4
1 tsp	black pepper	5 mL
	Salmon fillets with skin on (the marinade here is sufficient for about 5 to 10 lbs [2.5 to 5 kg] of fish)	

1. In a large shallow dish, combine whisky, oil, soy sauce, brown sugar, garlic and pepper. Add fish and marinate, flesh side down, in refrigerator for about 2 hours or overnight.

2. Oil grill or grill basket and barbecue skin side down for 7 to 10 minutes, until flesh flakes easily. For added flavor, add soaked alder or hickory chips to the barbecue. Place them in a foil pan and keep the lid down to smoke the fish. Serve immediately.

SERVES 4 TO 6

Tea-Smoked Trout

For an elegant appetizer, serve smoked trout on CORN AND SQUASH FRITTERS (see recipe, page 141) or WALNUT AND WILD RICE FRITTERS (see recipe, page 143) or squares of dark rye bread with a dollop of sour cream and a sprig of fresh dill.

4	8-oz [250 g] trout fillets, skin on *or* 1 whole lake trout (about 2 lbs [1 kg])	4
	Grated zest and juice of 1 lemon	
1 tbsp	coarse salt	15 mL
1/2 cup	loose Earl Grey or oolong tea	125 mL
1/2 cup	brown sugar	125 mL
1/4 tsp	black pepper	1 mL

1. Rub trout fillets or whole trout with salt, on both fleshy and skin sides. Place in a zippered plastic bag with lemon juice and zest and refrigerate overnight.

2. Line a heavy pan, large enough to hold the fish on a rack, with foil. (An old wok is good for this.) Sprinkle in the tea, brown sugar and pepper.

3. Set a rack over the tea, lay the fish on the rack and cover the pot tightly, first with foil, then with a lid or a dome of aluminum foil. Set over high heat. The sugar will melt and the pan will start smoking. Use an exhaust fan to vent the smoke from your kitchen or do this outside on the barbecue.

4. Smoke fillets for 10 minutes, 15 minutes for a whole fish. Let the trout stand in the covered pan for 10 minutes before removing the lid and foil. Serve hot or at room temperature.

Trout Primavera in Parchment

This is the way to serve trout in the spring, when the young asparagus spears — whether wild or cultivated — are poking up from their beds.

You can also wrap these packages in heavy foil to bake them. Or, wrap in foil and cook over campfire coals.

Try this recipe with other delicate fish fillets, like sole or perch.

PREHEAT OVEN TO 475° F (250° C)
PARCHMENT PAPER AND BAKING SHEETS

	Softened butter for coating paper	
12	stalks asparagus, trimmed and cut diagonally into 2-inch (5 cm) lengths	12
4	green onions, cut into julienne strips	4
2	carrots, cut into julienne strips	2
1	red pepper, cut into julienne strips	1
1/2 cup	chopped fresh parsley	125 mL
6	trout fillets (each about 8 oz [250 g]), skinned and boned	6
1/3 cup	lime juice	75 mL
1/3 cup	white wine	75 mL
3 tbsp	melted butter	45 mL
	Salt and pepper to taste	

1. Cut parchment paper into 6 pieces, each 10 by 20 inches (25 by 50 cm). Rub one side of the parchment paper with softened butter; fold in half to form a 10-inch (25 cm) square.

2. In a bowl combine asparagus, green onions, carrots, red pepper and parsley. Open each square of parchment paper; on one side, scatter half of the vegetables.

3. Rinse and dry fish fillets. Place one in each packet on top of vegetables. Drizzle fillets with lime juice, white wine and melted butter. Season with salt and pepper. Sprinkle with remaining vegetables.

4. Fold paper back over fish and seal securely by making small, overlapping folds or pleats around the edges. Place packets on baking sheet. Bake for 10 minutes per 1 inch (2.5 cm) thickness of fish. Packets will puff up and start to turn brown.

5. Transfer to individual plates and let your guests cut open the packets at the table. Or cut them open with kitchen shears or a sharp knife immediately before serving. Be careful: a blast of hot, fragrant steam will escape as you cut the paper.

SERVES 4

Poached Salmon with Red Wine Glaze

This dish makes a fast and elegant meal with wild rice or garlic mashed potatoes and sautéed red cabbage on the side.

2 lbs	salmon filet cut into 4 pieces	1 kg
1 cup	homemade fish stock *or* bottled clam stock	250 mL
1 cup	water	250 mL
1 tsp	whole black peppercorns	5 mL
1	sprig fresh thyme	1
2	sprigs fresh parsley	2

Glaze

1/2 cup	orange juice	125 mL
1 tbsp	brown sugar	15 mL
1/2 cup	dry red wine	125 mL
1 tbsp	balsamic vinegar	15 mL
1 tsp	tomato paste	5 mL
1 tbsp	butter	15 mL

1. In a wide skillet, combine stock, water, peppercorns, thyme and parsley; bring to a boil. Add salmon pieces, cover pan and reduce heat to low. Poach for 8 to 9 minutes or until salmon is firm and barely cooked.

2. Meanwhile, make the glaze: In a separate pan, combine orange juice, brown sugar, wine, vinegar and tomato paste. Bring to a boil and cook until reduced to about 1/3 cup (75 mL), about 5 minutes. Whisk in butter and keep warm.

3. Carefully remove salmon pieces from poaching liquid using a slotted spoon. Serve salmon with a drizzle of the red wine glaze.

eans are one dried staple you would find in every chuckwagon cook's traveling pantry. Every night the beans would be soaking and every day baked beans of some description would turn up at both breakfast and dinner. ✦ Some cooks carried white navy beans; others preferred red beans or pintos, clay-colored beauties with spots like a pinto pony. Any Cookie worth his salt could cook up a filling pot of beans, along with campfire biscuits, beef stew and coffee. In fact, beans were such an integral part of early cowboy fare that the call for grub might simply be, "The beans are on!" ✦ Chili has become so closely identified with cowboy cooking that no Western cookbook would be complete without a section devoted to this spicy concoction. Chili probably originated south of the border and migrated north to cowboy cooks as far as Canada, along with Texas cattle and cowboys. ✦ D.L. Jardine was one Texas chuckwagon cook who, legend has it, discovered it was easier to satisfy hungry cowhands if he spiced up the meat and beans from his chuck box with chilies and other savory spices. When he came upon local ingredients like peppers, cumin and oregano he added them to his repertoire, and Texas chili was born. ✦ In recent times, chili has acquired a new cachet and its preparation has even become a competitive sport. Every year, chili cooks vie for top honors at international chili cook-offs in Texas and California with their secret recipes containing

everything from cumin and ketchup to chocolate and beer. ✦ Here's a look at some interesting ways to cook up a mess of chili or a pot of beans. Some are dishes you can serve for breakfast with flapjacks and maple syrup; others are perfect alongside steak or make for a rib-sticking meal all by themselves. ✦ Cowboys called their beans "prairie strawberries" or "whistle berries" for obvious reasons. Or as one cowpuncher was heard to say, "I call them deceitful beans — 'cause they talk behind yore back."

Cowboy Chili and Baked Beans

Chuckwagon Beef Shortribs and Beans

SERVES 8 TO 10

Cluny-area rancher Leo Maynard gave me this recipe — the winner of a bean contest I once organized. (But then, how could he not win after he pulled into the newspaper parking lot with his chuckwagon and set up a wood stove to cook this tasty combination of Alberta beef and beans?) Leo also gave me my first taste of real prairie oysters, roasted over a campfire at a cowboy cooking contest — and another of my very favorite things, my orange kitty, O.J.

Leo serves this excellent chili with his own homemade biscuits.

If dried pinto beans are unavailable, use Romano or red kidney beans.

After browning ribs and cooking onions on the stove top, you can also put everything in a slow cooker and cook for 6 to 8 hours.

4 lbs	beef short ribs	2 kg
2 tbsp	canola oil	25 mL
4	chopped onions	4
1 lb	dried pinto beans (about 3 cups [750 mL]) soaked overnight in water to cover)	500 g
1	can (8 oz [213 mL]) tomato sauce	1
1/2 cup	packed brown sugar	125 mL
2 tbsp	prepared mustard	25 mL
2 tbsp	chili powder	25 mL
1 tbsp	cider vinegar	15 mL
2 tsp	liquid smoke	10 mL
1 tsp	Worcestershire sauce	5 mL
2 tsp	salt	10 mL

1. Cut ribs into pieces. In a large Dutch oven, heat oil over medium-high heat; in several batches, cook rib pieces for 5 minutes, turning occasionally, or until browned on all sides. With a slotted spoon, transfer ribs to a bowl leaving behind as much oil as possible. Reduce heat to medium; add onions and cook, stirring occasionally, for 8 minutes or until tender.

2. Stir in 6 cups (1.5 L) water, drained beans, tomato sauce, brown sugar, mustard, chili powder, vinegar, liquid smoke, Worcestershire sauce and half of the salt; bring to a boil. Place browned ribs on top, reduce heat to low, cover and simmer for 5 hours or until beans and ribs are tender. Season to taste with remaining salt.

Black Bean Chili

With earthy black beans, smoky chipotle chilies and a good shot of prairie rye whisky, this is truly an outstanding bean dish. Serve it over rice or rolled up in flour tortillas with chopped tomatoes and grated cheese.

3 tbsp	canola oil	45 mL
1	large onion, chopped	1
2 tbsp	paprika	25 mL
1 tbsp	dried oregano	15 mL
2 tsp	cumin seed	10 mL
1/4 tsp	cayenne pepper	1 mL
2 tsp	salt	10 mL
2	cloves garlic, minced	2
1	canned chipotle chili, chopped *or* 1 dried chipotle, rehydrated and chopped	1
1	chopped green pepper	1
1	can (28 oz [796 mL]) plum tomatoes, chopped	1
2 cups	dried black beans, soaked overnight in water to cover	500 mL
1/2 cup	rye whisky	125 mL
1	bay leaf	1
1/2 cup	chopped cilantro	125 mL
1 cup	shredded Cheddar cheese	250 mL
1 cup	sour cream, preferably low fat	250 mL
	Hot cooked rice as an accompaniment	

1. In a large saucepan, heat oil over medium heat. Add onion and cook for 5 minutes or until starting to brown. Stir in paprika, oregano, cumin seed and cayenne pepper; cook 2 minutes, stirring constantly. Stir in 1 tsp (5 mL) of the salt, garlic, chipotles, green pepper and tomatoes. Bring to a boil, reduce heat to medium-low and simmer, uncovered, for 15 minutes.

2. Stir in 3 cups (750 mL) water, drained beans, rye whisky and bay leaf. Bring to a boil, reduce heat to low and simmer, partially covered, for 2 to 3 hours or until beans are very tender.

3. Stir in cilantro. Season to taste with remaining salt. Serve over rice, topped with a sprinkling of grated cheese and a dollop of sour cream.

SERVES 6

Chicken and Sausage Chili

In summer, grill the sausage and chicken on the barbecue; use half the oil to brush the grill and half to cook the vegetables.

PREHEAT OVEN TO 350° F (180° C)

2 tbsp	olive oil	25 mL
1 lb	spicy Italian sausage	500 g
2	boneless skinless chicken breasts (about 8 oz [250 g]), cut into 1/2-inch (1 cm) cubes	2
1	onion, minced	1
2	cloves garlic, minced	2
1	red bell pepper, slivered	1
1	green pepper, slivered	1
2	jalapeno peppers, seeded and minced	2
1 3/4 cups	canned tomatoes with juices, chopped	425 mL
1 cup	chicken stock	250 mL
1/4 cup	cornmeal	50 mL
2 tbsp	chili powder	25 mL
1/2 tsp	ground cumin	2 mL
1/4 cup	chopped cilantro	50 mL
	Salt and pepper to taste	
	Hot sauce to taste	
3 cups	hot cooked rice	750 mL

1. In an ovenproof saucepan, heat 1 tbsp (15 mL) of the oil over medium-high heat; cook sausages, turning occasionally, for 5 minutes or until well-browned. Remove from saucepan, leaving behind as much oil as possible. Add chicken to saucepan; cook for 5 minutes or until well-browned and cooked through. Remove chicken from pan; set aside, keeping separate from sausage. Cut sausage diagonally into 1/2-inch (1 cm) slices.

2. In the same saucepan, heat remaining oil over medium-high heat; add onion, garlic, red and green peppers and jalapenos; cook, stirring occasionally, for 3 minutes or until softened. Stir in tomatoes, chicken stock, cornmeal, chili powder and cumin; bring to a boil, stirring constantly. Add cooked sausage, cover and transfer to oven. Bake for 50 minutes. Stir in chicken; bake 5 minutes longer.

3. Stir in cilantro. Season to taste with salt, pepper and hot sauce. Serve over rice.

Pork and Beef Chili with Ancho Sauce

SERVES 8

Dutch ovens are cast iron pots that can be suspended above the fire or set right down into the fire on their stubby legs and surrounded by coals. More coals are piled on the lids and the ovens left to "bake" their contents, whether they be biscuits, roasts or loaves of bread.

Cooking over a campfire in a Dutch oven is not easy. Many cowboy cooks report campfire cooking disasters, from charred biscuit and scorched stews to petrified eggs, coming from these big cast iron pots. The best advice, says one cook, is to use good hardwood to build your fire. Oak, hickory, maple or mesquite will all provide good heat-holding coals for hours of cooking while soft woods like cedar, aspen or popular make for poor, inconsistent heat and bitter smoke.

2	dried ancho chilies	2
1/4 cup	olive oil	50 mL
1 lb	pork shoulder stew meat, cut into 1/2-inch (1 cm) cubes	500 g
1 lb	beef chuck steak, cut into 1/4- to 1/2-inch (5 mm to 1 cm) cubes	500 g
1	large onion, chopped	1
5	cloves garlic, minced	5
4 oz	spicy Italian sausage, casings removed	125 g
1 tbsp	ground cumin	15 mL
1 tbsp	crushed hot chilies	15 mL
2	cans (each 19 oz [540 mL]) tomatoes, chopped	2
1/4 cup	rye whisky	50 mL
1 tbsp	dried oregano	15 mL
1 1/2 cups	cooked black beans	375 mL
1/4 cup	tomato paste	50 mL
	Salt and pepper to taste	

1. Soak ancho chilies in hot water 20 minutes or until softened; drain. Chop, discarding stems and seeds; set aside.

2. In a large Dutch oven, heat oil over medium-high heat. In several batches, cook diced pork and beef, turning often, for 4 minutes or until well-browned. With a slotted spoon, transfer to a bowl leaving behind as much oil as possible; set aside. Reduce heat to medium-low. Add onions, garlic and sausage; cook, stirring to break up meat, for 4 minutes or until onion is softened and meat is no longer pink. Stir in ancho chilies, cumin and crushed chilies; cook for 5 minutes or until onion is tender.

3. Stir in browned pork and beef, tomatoes, whisky and oregano. Bring to a boil. Reduce heat to low and simmer, covered, for 1 1/2 hours.

4. Stir in beans and tomato paste. Simmer 15 minutes longer to heat through. Season to taste with salt and pepper.

Wagon Boss Chili

This chili is served at an Alberta guest ranch, where you can recall the days of the big cattle drives, complete with thousands of head of cattle and mounted cowboys, led by the wagon boss.

When cowboy cooks first put meat and peppers together, the seeds of modern-day chili were sown and the West became the official domain of chili, hot sauces, searing salsas and chiliheads.

Substitute Romano beans or red kidney beans if you can't find pinto beans.

2 lbs	lean round steak, cut into 1/2-inch (1 cm) cubes	1 kg
2 tbsp	canola oil	25 mL
3	cloves garlic, minced	3
2 cups	chopped onions	500 mL
2 cups	beef broth	500 mL
2 cups	canned tomatoes with juices, chopped	500 mL
2 tbsp	chili powder	25 mL
1 tsp	dried oregano	5 mL
1 tsp	ground cumin	5 mL
1/2 tsp	cayenne pepper	2 mL
1/2 tsp	salt	2 mL
1/4 tsp	freshly ground black pepper	1 mL
1	can (19 oz [540 mL]) pinto beans, rinsed and drained	1
3 tbsp	cornmeal	45 mL

1. In a Dutch oven, heat oil over medium-high heat. In several batches, cook beef, turning occasionally, for 5 minutes or until well-browned. Return all beef to saucepan, along with garlic and onions; cook for 5 minutes or until onions are tender.

2. Stir in the 1 cup (250 mL) water, beef broth, tomatoes, chili powder, oregano, cumin, cayenne pepper, salt and pepper. Bring to a boil, reduce heat to low and simmer, covered, for 2 hours or until meat is very tender.

3. Stir in beans and cornmeal; simmer for another 20 minutes or until mixture is heated through and thickened.

SERVES 8

Maple Baked Pork and Beans with Caramelized Apples

This recipe makes a delicious old-fashioned bean dish, good alongside your barbecue beef on a bun — or even with pancakes — for a Stampede breakfast. It's a variation of a recipe Calgarian Rick Gauthier entered in a bean contest and for which he won second place.

12-CUP (3 L) BEAN POT *OR* CASSEROLE DISH

2 cups	dried navy beans, rinsed	500 mL
1 tbsp	molasses	15 mL
8 oz	back bacon, preferably double-smoked	250 g
4	Granny Smith apples	4
1	large onion, chopped	1
1/2 cup	maple syrup	125 mL
1 tbsp	dry mustard	15 mL
1 tsp	coarse salt	5 mL
1/4 cup	butter	50 mL
1/4 cup	packed brown sugar	50 mL
1/2 cup	rum	125 mL

1. In a saucepan combine beans, molasses and 8 cups (2 L) water; bring to a boil. Remove from heat; let stand, covered, for 1 hour. Uncover. Bring to a boil, reduce heat to low and simmer, covered, for 45 minutes to 1 hour or until beans are starting to get tender. Drain.

2. Preheat oven to 325° F (160° C). Chop bacon into thin slivers. Peel and chop 2 of the apples. In a bean pot, combine drained beans, bacon, chopped apples, onions, maple syrup, mustard and salt. Cover and bake for 3 hours. Stir; if beans seem dry, add a little hot water. Cover and bake 1 to 2 hours longer.

3. Meanwhile, core remaining apples and slice into 1/2-inch (1 cm) rings. In a frying pan, melt butter over medium heat. Stir in brown sugar; cook for 2 minutes, stirring occasionally. Add apple rings, stirring to coat with sugar. Add half of the rum; increase heat to medium-high and cook 8 minutes, turning rings occasionally, or until the liquid evaporates and apples are tender. Set aside.

4. Remove cover from bean pot and arrange caramelized apple slices on top of the beans. Bake, uncovered, for 30 minutes longer. Just before serving, pour the remaining rum slowly over the beans.

SERVES 10

Prairie Fire Beans

Dried beans keep indefinitely and, when eaten with rice or other grains, are a complete protein — high in fiber and complex carbohydrates, as well as low in fat.

In Texas and Mexico, red beans or mottled pinto beans are most common and are the basis for most chili dishes. Further north, the Great Northern bean is grown. This large white bean is the North American version of the Haricot bean or Italian Cannellini bean. Navy or pea beans are smaller white beans, used for pots of molasses-spiked baked beans or in soups. Heirloom beans like Tongues of Fire, Anasazi, flageolots and Rattlesnakes have taken on a new cachet as today's western cooks search for healthier ways to cut down on fat and protein in their traditionally meat-based diets.

2 lbs	dried pinto beans (about 5 cups [1.25 L]), soaked overnight in water to cover	1 kg
1	large ham hock or ham bone	1
1	small whole onion, peeled	1
Pinch	salt	Pinch
2 tbsp	butter	25 mL
1 lb	sharp Cheddar cheese, shredded	500 g
1 tsp	Prairie Fire hot sauce or other hot sauce	5 mL
1 cup	finely chopped onions	250 mL
2	cloves garlic, minced	2
	Additional hot sauce to taste	
	Salt and pepper to taste	

1. In a large saucepan, combine drained beans, ham hock, whole onion and a pinch of salt. Add cold water to cover beans by 2 inches (5 cm). Bring to a boil, reduce heat to low and simmer, covered, for 1 hour or until beans are tender.

2. Discard ham hock and onion. Drain beans; return to saucepan. Stir in butter, cheese, hot sauce, onions and garlic. Cook, covered, over low heat for 20 minutes or until cheese melts and everything is tender.

3. Season to taste with additional hot sauce, salt and pepper.

Vegetarian Chili

This recipe comes from a cafe in Calgary called The Breadline. It's easy to make and chock full of healthy vegetables. Although you probably won't find many vegetarian cowboys, this is a very tasty chili, very low in fat, and excellent as a meatless dinner or side dish.

1/3 cup	olive oil	75 mL
1 lb	zucchini, cut into 1/2-inch (1 cm) dice	500 g
1 lb	onions, cut into 1/2-inch (1 cm) dice	500 g
4	cloves garlic, minced	4
1	large red pepper, chopped	1
2	cans (each 28 oz [796 mL]) tomatoes, crushed	2
1 1/2 lbs	cubed ripe tomatoes (about 4 cups[1 L]) chopped)	750 g
4 tsp	chili powder	20 mL
1 tbsp	ground cumin	15 mL
1 tbsp	dried basil	15 mL
1 tbsp	dried oregano	15 mL
1 1/2 tsp	freshly ground pepper	7 mL
1 tsp	salt	5 mL
1 tsp	fennel seed	5 mL
2 tbsp	chopped fresh parsley	25 mL
1	can (19 oz [540 mL]) red kidney beans, rinsed and drained	1
1	can (14 oz [398 mL]) chickpeas, rinsed and drained	1
1 tbsp	chopped fresh dill	15 mL
1 tbsp	lemon juice	15 mL
3/4 tsp	granulated sugar	4 mL

1. In a large saucepan, heat olive oil over medium-high heat. Add zucchini, onion, garlic and peppers; cook, stirring often, for 8 minutes or until starting to soften. Stir in canned and fresh tomatoes, chili powder, cumin, basil, oregano, pepper, salt, fennel seed and parsley; bring to a boil. Reduce heat to medium and simmer, uncovered and stirring often, for 30 minutes.

2. Stir in kidney beans, chickpeas, dill, lemon juice and sugar; cook 15 minutes longer.

Prairie Bean Cassoulet

Beans from Taber, Alberta, combined with lamb and old-fashioned Ukrainian or Italian sausage are featured in this simplified prairie version of a traditional French dish. Enjoy it after a day of skiing, served with lots of mashed potatoes.

After Step 2, layer the beans, meat mixture and sausage in a slow cooker, adding liquid as necessary. Cook on low heat for 12 hours. Turn cassoulet into casserole dish and proceed with Step 4.

14-CUP (3.5 L) BEAN POT, CASSEROLE DISH OR ROASTING PAN

1 lb	dried navy beans (about 2 1/4 cups [550 mL]), rinsed	500 g
8 oz	bacon (preferably double-smoked), chopped	250 g
1 tsp	coarse salt	5 mL
1 tsp	chopped fresh thyme	5 mL
1 tsp	chopped fresh rosemary	5 mL
1 tsp	freshly ground black pepper	5 mL
2	cloves garlic, minced	2
1 1/2 lbs	lamb or pork shoulder, cut into 1-inch (2.5 cm) cubes	750 g
2 tbsp	canola oil	25 mL
1 cup	chopped onions	250 mL
1	ripe tomato, chopped	1
2 tbsp	tomato paste	25 mL
1/2 tsp	ground cloves	2 mL
1 lb	kielbasa *or* Italian sausage	500 g

Topping

1 cup	dry bread crumbs	250 mL
1/4 cup	melted butter	50 mL
2 tbsp	chopped fresh parsley	25 mL
1/2 tsp	freshly ground black pepper	2 mL
2	cloves garlic, minced	2

1. In a large saucepan, combine beans and 3 cups (750 mL) water; bring to a boil. Remove from heat; let stand, covered, for 40 minutes. Drain. Put half of the bacon in the bottom of the saucepan; top with drained beans. Add salt and 4 cups (1 L) of water. Bring to a boil, reduce heat to low and simmer, covered, for 1 1/2 hours or until tender. Drain beans, reserving cooking liquid. Set beans and bean cooking liquid aside.

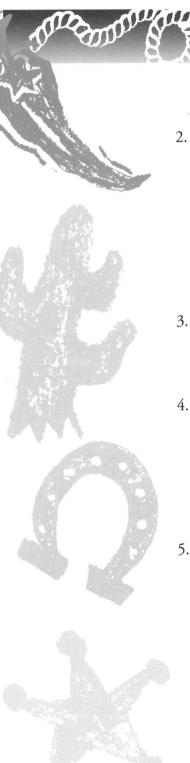

2. Meanwhile, mix the thyme, rosemary, pepper and garlic; rub over the cubed lamb or pork. In a large frying pan, heat oil over medium-high heat; in batches, cook meat, turning occasionally, for 5 minutes or until well browned. With a slotted spoon, transfer meat to a bowl, leaving behind as much oil as possible. Cook remaining bacon and onions for 4 minutes or until onions are translucent. Stir in browned meat, tomato, tomato paste and cloves; set aside.

3. In a nonstick frying pan sprayed with vegetable spray, cook Italian sausage, if using, over medium-high heat, turning occasionally, for 5 minutes or until browned. Cut kielbasa or browned Italian sausage into chunks; set aside.

4. Preheat oven to 300° F (150° C). In roasting pan, layer one-third of the beans, one-third of the meat mixture and one-third of the sausage; repeat layers twice. Add just enough of the bean cooking liquid to come to the top layer of beans, adding extra water if necessary. Bake, covered, for 2 hours or until meat is tender. Remove from oven. Increase oven heat to 350° F (180° C).

5. In a bowl stir together bread crumbs, butter, parsley, pepper and garlic. Sprinkle over cassoulet. Bake, uncovered, for 20 minutes, or until topping is golden brown.

You may not find many vegetarian cowhands, but eating large portions of meat everyday is losing its shine — even out West. This section offers some newfangled recipes for meals without meat, using old-fashioned staples like beans and Indian fry bread in updated recipes like tostadas or new gourmet fillings for simple potato perogies. Even cowboys need to eat their veggies, so there are plenty of ideas for vegetable side dishes using prairie ingredients such as potatoes, root vegetables, cabbage, wild rice and corn, along with grain-based pilafs to serve along with your chili or ribs. So get ready to try some vegetable dishes — all prepared with Wild West flair.

Vegetables and Side Dishes

Indian Frybread Tostadas

rybread or bannock is always found at Native powwows and at rodeos like the Calgary Stampede, where you can have it hot and sprinkled with sugar. Natives throughout the West, from prairie Blackfoot tribes to the Navajo in Arizona, rely on frybread as a daily staple. This dish is a kind of tostada, with beans (or you can use ground beef), lettuce, tomatoes, cheese and guacamole piled high on a piece of warm frybread.

Frybread

3 cups	all-purpose flour (or half white and half whole wheat)	750 mL
1 tsp	baking powder	5 mL
1 tsp	salt	5 mL
Pinch	granulated sugar (optional)	Pinch
1 cup	warm milk	250 mL
1 tsp	canola oil	5 mL
	Canola oil for frying	

Toppings

1 tbsp	canola oil	15 mL
2	cloves garlic, minced	2
1	onion, chopped	1
1	green pepper, chopped	1
2	cans (each 19 oz [540 mL]) pinto beans, rinsed and drained	2
1/4 cup	tomato sauce, ketchup or bottled barbecue sauce	50 mL
1 tbsp	chili powder	15 mL
1 tsp	ground cumin	5 mL
1 cup	shredded lettuce	250 mL
1 cup	chopped tomato	250 mL
1 cup	shredded sharp Cheddar	250 mL
1/2 cup	low-fat sour cream	125 mL
1/4 cup	sliced black olives	50 mL
1/4 cup	chopped cilantro	50 mL
1/4 cup	chopped green onions	50 mL

1. Frybread: In a large bowl, stir together flour, baking powder, salt and, if using, sugar. Stir in the warm milk and oil, mixing with a wooden spoon. Stir in just enough warm water to make a soft but not sticky dough, up to 1/2 cup (125 mL). Divide dough into 8 equal pieces. Shape each piece into a 6-inch (15 cm) round, stretching and flattening dough with your hands. In a heavy frying pan, heat 1/2-inch (1 cm) canola oil over medium-high heat. One at a time, fry dough rounds 1 to 2 minutes per side or until golden brown. Drain on paper towels.

2. Topping: In a frying pan, heat oil over medium-high heat. Add garlic, onion and green pepper; cook 5 minutes or until tender. Stir in beans, tomato sauce, chili powder and cumin; cook, stirring, 2 minutes or until heated through.

3. Place frybreads on individual plates. Pile some shredded lettuce on each piece of frybread, then top with some warm bean mixture, chopped tomato and cheddar. Place a dollop of sour cream on the top of the tostadas, and sprinkle each with some sliced black olives, cilantro and green onion.

Black Bean and Cornmeal Torta

A great combination of two prairie ingredients — beans and cornmeal — this rib-sticking vegetarian dish will feed a crowd at your next picnic or brunch. Serve it hot or cold, as an appetizer or main dish.

PREHEAT OVEN TO 350° F (180° C)
10-INCH (3 L) SPRINGFORM PAN

Bean layer

2 tsp	olive oil	10 mL
1	onion, chopped	1
2	jalapeno peppers, seeded and minced	2
1 tbsp	chopped garlic	15 mL
2 cups	cooked black beans	500 mL
	Salt and pepper to taste	

Onion layer

1 tbsp	olive oil	15 mL
4	onions, cut into slivers	4
2	dried pasilla chilies, rehydrated, stemmed, seeded and chopped	2
2	red bell peppers, thinly sliced	2

Polenta layer

1 1/2 cups	cornmeal	375 mL
2 tbsp	butter	25 mL
1 tbsp	minced garlic	15 mL
1 tbsp	chopped fresh basil	15 mL
3/4 tsp	salt	4 mL
1/4 tsp	pepper	1 mL
5	large (10-inch [25 cm]) whole wheat tortillas	5
1 lb	Monterey Jack cheese, thinly sliced	500 g
	Sour cream and salsa as toppings	

Recipe continues...

TROUT PRIMAVERA IN PARCHMENT (PAGE 110) ➤
OVERLEAF: MAPLE BAKED PORK AND BEANS WITH CARAMELIZED APPLES (PAGE 119)

1. Bean layer: In a frying pan, heat oil over medium heat. Add onion, jalapenos and garlic; cook 8 minutes or until tender. Stir in black beans. Season to taste with salt and pepper. Set aside.

2. Onion layer: In a saucepan heat oil over medium heat; add onions and cook, stirring often, 15 minutes or until tender and golden. Stir in chilies and peppers; cook 10 minutes longer or until peppers are tender. Set aside.

3. Polenta: In a deep, heavy saucepan, bring 6 cups (1.5 L) water to a boil. Reduce heat to low. Slowly add cornmeal in a thin steady stream, whisking until smooth. Stir in butter, garlic, basil and salt and pepper. Cook over low heat for 30 minutes, stirring constantly, or until mixture comes away from sides of pan.

4. Assembly: Place a flour tortilla in bottom of springform pan. Top with half of the warm polenta, spreading it over surface. Layer with half of the onion mixture and one-quarter of the cheese. Top with another tortilla; press down. Layer with half of the beans, one-quarter of the cheese, a tortilla, remaining beans, one-quarter of the cheese and another tortilla; press down. Layer with remaining polenta, remaining onions and a tortilla; press down. Top with remaining cheese. Bake torta for 30 minutes or until browned and bubbly. Cool slightly and remove sides from springform pan. Serve warm or at room temperature, cut into wedges with a little sour cream and salsa on the side.

< INDIAN FRYBREAD TOSTADAS (PAGE 126)

Perogies with Potato, Wild Mushroom and Two-Cheese Filling

The old-fashioned prairie perogy is a staple for several of our founding ethnic groups — Ukrainian, Polish, Romanian, German and Austrian. The potatoes in the dough make these dumplings particularly fluffy.

You can make several batches of perogies and freeze them for cooking later. Set uncooked perogies on cookie sheets lined with plastic and freeze in a single layer. When frozen, pop the dumplings into zippered freezer bags. To cook, drop frozen perogies into a large pot of boiling water. Return water to a gentle boil (be careful not to boil too vigorously or the dumplings may disintegrate). Perogies are cooked through when they rise to the top and float.

BAKING SHEETS LINED WITH WAXED PAPER

Dough

4 cups	all-purpose flour	1 L
2 cups	cold mashed potatoes	500 mL
3 tbsp	vegetable shortening *or* butter	45 mL
1 tsp	salt	5 mL
1	egg	1

Mushroom Filling...

1 tbsp	butter	15 mL
1	small onion, minced	1
1	clove garlic, minced	1
1 oz	dried wild mushrooms, rehydrated and minced	25 g
3 cups	cold mashed potatoes	750 mL
1 cup	mixed grated cheese (such as old Cheddar, blue and Fontina)	250 mL
	Salt and pepper to taste	

...*or* Cheese Filling

3 cups	cold mashed potatoes	750 mL
1/2 cup	shredded old Cheddar	125 mL
1/2 cup	creamed cottage cheese	125 mL

Salt and pepper to taste

Low-fat sour cream mixed with minced green onion and/or sliced onions fried in butter as toppings

Start by peeling and boiling about 3 lbs (1.5 kg) potatoes to get the 5 cups (1.25 L) of mashed potatoes you'll need for dough and whichever filling you choose.

1. Dough: In a large bowl, combine flour, mashed potatoes, shortening and salt, mixing with your hands until mealy. In a liquid measuring cup, beat egg; add enough luke-warm water to make 1 cup (250 mL). Mix well into potato mixture, adding just enough extra warm water to make a smooth, not sticky, dough. Let rest 15 minutes.

2. If making Mushroom Filling: In a saucepan, melt butter over medium heat. Add onion, garlic and mushrooms; cook 6 minutes or until tender. Mix in mashed potatoes and shredded cheese. Season to taste with salt and pepper. Cool.

3. If making Cheese Filling: In a bowl stir together mashed potatoes, Cheddar and cottage cheese until well combined. Season to taste with salt and pepper. Set aside.

4. Assembly: Divide dough into 4 equal pieces. On a lightly floured board, roll the pieces one at a time to 1/4-inch (5 mm) thickness. Using a cookie cutter or rim of a glass, cut into 2 1/2-inch (6 cm) circles. Fill each with 2 tsp (10 mL) of filling, stretch dough over to form a half-moon shape and pinch edges together to seal. Repeat with remaining dough and filling, placing perogies on waxed paper-lined baking sheets as they are filled.

5. To cook, drop dumplings into a large pot of salted boiling water. Cook for 3 minutes, stirring gently to make sure none stick to the bottom, or until they rise to the top. Drain. Serve topped with fried onions or low-fat sour cream and green onions.

SERVES 4

Potato Enchiladas

Using spiced potatoes as a filling for these vegetarian enchiladas is an unusual but delicious way to use local potatoes in a popular Western dish.

If corn tortillas are unavailable in your area, use flour tortillas — since they're soft you won't need to heat them in a frying pan before stuffing.

13- BY 9-INCH (3 L) BAKING DISH, OILED
PREHEAT OVEN TO 400° F (200° C)

Filling

6	large potatoes (about 2 lbs [1 kg]), peeled, boiled and mashed	6
10 oz	strong cheese (such as feta or old Cheddar), crumbled or shredded	300 g
1 1/2 cups	low-fat sour cream	375 mL
6	green onions, chopped	6
4	jalapeno peppers, roasted, peeled, seeded and chopped	4
1 tbsp	chili powder	15 mL
	Salt and pepper to taste	
10	large (10-inch [25 cm]) corn tortillas *or* 20 small (6-inch [15 cm]) corn tortillas	10

Sauce

6	canned tomatoes, chopped	6
2	cloves garlic, minced	2
2	jalapeno peppers, seeded and minced	2
1	mild chili pepper, roasted, seeded and peeled	1
1 cup	chicken stock	250 mL
1/2 cup	chopped cilantro	125 mL
2 tbsp	fresh lime juice	25 mL
4 oz	mozzarella or old Cheddar cheese, shredded	125 g

1. Filling: In a large bowl, combine mashed potatoes, cheese, sour cream, green onion, jalapeno pepper and chili powder. Season to taste with salt and pepper.

2. Heat a heavy frying pan (preferably cast iron) over medium heat. Warm tortillas in pan one at a time, turning frequently until soft and pliable; fill tortillas with 2/3 cup (150 mL) filling and roll up. (If using small tortillas, fill with 1/3 cup (75 mL) filling.) Place seam-side down in baking dish.

3. Sauce: In a blender combine tomatoes, garlic, jalapenos, chili pepper, chicken stock, cilantro and lime juice; purée until smooth. Pour into a saucepan. Bring to a boil; cook 5 minutes or until slightly thickened. Pour sauce over tortillas. Sprinkle with shredded cheese. Bake for 10 minutes or until heated through and cheese is melted.

Cowboy Pasta
with Ranchero Sauce

SERVES 4

Pasta is a modern word in the cowboy vocabulary, but today most ranch cooks will include spaghetti sauces and lasagnas in their everyday fare. This spicy sauce is meatless and is great on all kinds of noodles. Or try it ladled into an omelet, added to a flour tortilla wrap with grilled meats and vegetables, or spooned over pan-fried chicken breasts. Serve it up with your favorite spaghetti western!

Use 12 oz (375 g) dried pasta to replace 1 lb (500 g) fresh.

16	plum tomatoes (about 4 lbs [2 kg]), cored and halved	16
12	serrano chilies, halved, stemmed and seeded	12
2	onions (preferably Vidalia), sliced	2
12	cloves garlic, peeled	12
1 cup	beer	250 mL
1/4 cup	olive oil	50 mL
1 cup	cilantro leaves	250 mL
1 tsp	salt	5 mL

Pasta

1 lb	fresh pasta, any shape	500 g
4 oz	feta cheese, dry ricotta or aged goat cheese, crumbled	125g
2 tbsp	chopped cilantro	25 mL
2	green onions, chopped	2

1. Sauce: In a large saucepan, bring 6 cups (1.5 L) water to a boil. Add tomatoes, serranos, onions and 6 cloves of the garlic. Reduce heat to medium and simmer, uncovered, for 30 minutes. Drain, reserving liquid. In a food processor, combine solids, 2 cups (500 mL) of reserved cooking liquid and beer; purée until smooth.

2. Wipe out saucepan. Add oil and heat over medium heat; add 4 cloves of the garlic and cook for 5 minutes or until browned. Discard garlic. Add puréed sauce to oil. Reduce heat to medium-low and simmer, uncovered, for 30 minutes. Mince remaining 2 cloves of garlic with cilantro; stir into sauce along with salt. Simmer 20 minutes longer.

3. In a large pot of boiling, salted water, cook pasta until *al dente*. Drain and toss with about half of the sauce or enough to coat. (Save remaining sauce for another use.) Add crumbled cheese, cilantro and green onions and toss again. Serve immediately.

Spring Greens Pie

Real cowboys may not reach quiche, but they'll love this hearty spinach pie filled with spring greens. When there's arugula and spinach in the garden, and young dandelions in the lawn, this tasty dish makes a great breakfast, lunch or fast supper. Without the crust, it's also relatively low in fat.

PREHEAT OVEN TO 375° F (190° C)
9-INCH (23 CM) PIE PLATE

2 tbsp	olive oil	25 mL
1	onion, minced	1
2	cloves garlic, minced	2
12 cups	chopped Swiss chard (about 1 1/2 lbs [750 g])	3 L
5 cups	chopped arugula (about 8 oz [250 g])	1.25 L
4 1/2 cups	chopped dandelion greens (about 12 oz [375 g])	1.125 L
2	small zucchini, grated	2
Half	yellow bell pepper, chopped	Half
1/2 cup	chopped fresh parsley	125 mL
1/3 cup	chopped fresh basil	75 mL
1/2 tsp	salt	2 mL
1/4 tsp	freshly ground black pepper	1 mL
3	extra large eggs, lightly beaten	3
1/4 cup	freshly grated Parmesan cheese	50 mL
1/4 cup	shredded Swiss cheese	50 mL
1/4 cup	fresh bread crumbs	50 mL

1. In a large saucepan or stock pot, heat 1 tbsp (5 mL) of the oil over medium heat. Add onion and garlic; cook for 5 minutes or until tender. Stir in Swiss chard, arugula, dandelion greens, zucchini, yellow pepper, parsley, basil, salt and pepper; cover and cook for 10 minutes, stirring occasionally, or until tender.

2. Remove cover and cook, stirring often, for 20 minutes longer or until all liquid is evaporated. Transfer to a bowl and cool slightly.

3. Beat the eggs into the greens and pour into pie plate. Sprinkle with cheeses. Mix bread crumbs with remaining tablespoon of oil, then sprinkle over pie. Bake for 25 to 30 minutes. Let stand at least 10 minutes before serving.

Grain-Zucchini Casserole with Cheese Topping

SERVES 6

The bulgar used in this recipe can also be cooked as a breakfast cereal, in baked goods, pilafs and substituted for rice or pasta as a base for sauces and stews. Mix hydrated bulgar with ground meat as an extender for hamburgers and stuffings. Medium or coarse ground bulgar is best in cooked dishes and pilafs, while finely ground bulgar works well in uncooked dishes where the grain is merely soaked. Keep dry bulgar wheat indefinitely in a cool, dark cupboard.

You can substitute 1/2 tsp (2 mL) dried herbs for each 1 tbsp (15 mL) fresh used in this recipe.

PREHEAT OVEN TO 350° F (180° C)
10-CUP (2.5 L) CASSEROLE DISH, OILED

1 cup	bulgar *or* coarse cracked wheat	250 mL
1 tbsp	canola oil	15 mL
2 cups	sliced onions	500 mL
4	cloves garlic, minced	4
1 1/4 lbs	zucchini, halved lengthwise and sliced thinly (about 6 cups [1.5 L])	625 g
1 cup	chopped fresh parsley	250 mL
2 tbsp	tomato paste	25 mL
1 tbsp	soy sauce	15 mL
1/2 tsp	freshly ground black pepper	2 mL
1 tbsp	chopped fresh basil	15 mL
1 tbsp	chopped fresh marjoram	15 mL
1 tbsp	chopped fresh oregano	15 mL
2	eggs, lightly beaten	2
1 cup	crumbled feta cheese	250 mL
1 cup	low-fat ricotta cheese *or* 1% cottage cheese	250 mL
2	tomatoes, sliced	2
	Salt and pepper to taste	

1. In a small saucepan, bring 1 1/2 cups (375 mL) water to a boil. Stir in bulgar and remove from heat. Let stand, covered, for 15 minutes.

2. Meanwhile, in a saucepan heat oil over medium heat. Add onions and garlic; cook for 5 minutes or until tender. Stir in zucchini; cover and cook 8 minutes or until tender. Stir into rehydrated bulgar along with parsley, tomato paste, soy sauce and pepper. In a small bowl, mix together basil, marjoram and oregano; stir 2 tbsp (25 mL) of the mixture into bulgar, reserving rest for topping. Turn bulgar mixture into prepared casserole dish.

3. In a bowl whisk eggs with feta and ricotta cheese (or process in food processor) until smooth. Pour over top of casserole. Top with sliced tomatoes and sprinkle with salt, pepper and reserved herbs. Bake uncovered for 45 minutes. Let stand for 10 minutes before serving.

SERVES 6

Garlic Mashed Spuds

Why didn't someone think of this long ago? These spuds are so easy and so sublime.

Roasting the garlic will enhance sweetness and flavor. For roasting procedure, see Step 1 of Caesar Salad recipe on page 55. Add roasted garlic when mashing potatoes.

8	large Yukon Gold potatoes, peeled and quartered	8
4	cloves garlic, peeled	4
1/2 cup	milk	125 mL
2 tbsp	butter	25 mL
	Salt and pepper to taste	

1. In a saucepan combine potatoes and garlic. Add cold salted water to cover. Bring to a boil, cover, reduce heat to medium and simmer 20 minutes or until tender.
2. Drain potatoes and garlic. Mash with milk, butter and salt and pepper to taste. (Add more milk if you prefer your potatoes creamier.)

SERVES 6

Roasted Root Vegetables with Wild Mint

You can find wild mint growing along gravelly streams and you will likely smell its fragrance before you see it. Mint grows well in Alberta gardens and is a perennial you can enjoy every spring and summer. Try this flavorful herb in sauces for lamb, chopped up and sprinkled over sweet new potatoes or with fresh young peas.

PREHEAT OVEN TO 400° F (200° C)
ROASTING PAN *OR* RIMMED BAKING SHEET

6	new potatoes, cut into chunks	6
3	carrots, cut into chunks	3
2	parsnips, cut into chunks	2
1	red onion, quartered	1
2 tbsp	olive oil	25 mL
2 tbsp	chopped fresh mint, preferably wild	25 mL
1 tsp	lemon juice	5 mL
	Salt and pepper to taste	

1. In a large bowl, toss together potatoes, carrots, parsnips, onion and olive oil. Spread vegetables out in single layer in roasting pan or on baking sheet.
2. Roast about 1 hour, turning occasionally, or until tender and caramelized. Stir in fresh mint and lemon juice. Season to taste with salt and pepper.

Baked Stuffed Potatoes with Roots and Ginger

SERVES 4

On most ranches in the Old West, families relied on what they could produce themselves. Summer gardens provided fresh produce for canning and enough potatoes, carrots, parsnips and turnips to fill the root cellars for the winter. Here's a dish that shows root vegetables at their finest.

PREHEAT OVEN TO 400° F (200° C)

2	large baking potatoes	2
2	carrots, cut into chunks	2
1	parsnip, cut into chunks	1
1/4 cup	butter	50 mL
3	green onions, minced	3
1 tbsp	minced ginger root	15 mL
1/4 cup	milk *or* cream	50 mL
	Salt and pepper to taste	

1. Scrub potatoes and prick skins with a fork. Bake for 1 hour or until soft.

2. Meanwhile, put carrots and parsnip in a microwave-safe dish with 1 tbsp (15 mL) water, cover and microwave on High for 4 minutes or until tender. Drain and set aside.

3. Cut each potato in half lengthwise and scoop out flesh, leaving about 1/4-inch (5 mm) shell. Mash potato flesh roughly with cooked vegetables, so some small pieces of carrot and parsnip remain.

4. In a frying pan, melt butter over medium heat. Add green onions and ginger; cook for 5 minutes or until tender. Stir into mashed vegetables, along with milk. Season to taste with salt and pepper. Pile mashed vegetable mixture back into potato shells. Bake for 10 minutes or microwave on High for 3 minutes or until heated through.

Braised Red Cabbage with Bacon and Apples

SERVES 6

For early settlers, trips to the nearest settlement for supplies might only be taken twice a year, so staples were simple — flour, sugar, honey, molasses, rice, oatmeal, barrels of apples in the fall and dried fruit. Everything else was produced on the ranch, including the bacon, onions and cabbage featured in this recipe.

4	slices bacon	4
1	onion, cut into slivers	1
2	Granny Smith apples, peeled and sliced	2
1	medium red cabbage (about 3 lbs [1.5kg]), cored and shredded	1
2 tbsp	brown sugar	25 mL
2 tbsp	wine vinegar	25 mL
1 tbsp	grainy mustard	15 mL
	Salt and pepper to taste	

1. In a large saucepan set over medium heat, cook bacon 8 minutes or until crisp. Remove from pan; crumble and set aside. Add the onion and apples to the pan; cook for 5 minutes or until tender. Stir in brown sugar, vinegar and mustard.

2. Stir in cabbage and 1/2 cup (125 mL) water. Simmer, uncovered, for 15 minutes, stirring frequently, or until cabbage is tender. Stir in crumbled bacon. Season to taste with salt and pepper.

Roasted Beets with Warm Dill Sauce

Pickled beets were a staple in most old-time prairie pantries. Here's a take on fresh beets, that's reminiscent of that old-fashioned flavor.

PREHEAT OVEN TO 350° F (180° C)

12	small beets, scrubbed	12
1/3 cup	white wine vinegar	75 mL
2 tbsp	granulated sugar	25 mL
1 tbsp	chopped fresh dill	15 mL

1. Wrap beets individually in foil. Bake for 1 hour or until tender. Cool beets slightly, then slip off skins and slice.

2. In a small saucepan, combine vinegar and sugar; cook over medium-high heat for 1 minute or until sugar is dissolved. Toss with warm beets. Sprinkle with fresh dill and serve immediately.

Herbed Whole Wheat Toss

There are so many flour mills and cereal producers across the western prairies it's hard to list them all. Alberta's Prairie Sun Grains Ltd. is one that processes a variety of grain products, including the whole wheat kernels used here.

2 cups	whole wheat kernels (wheat berries), preferably Durham wheat	500 mL
2 tbsp	butter	25 mL
1/4 cup	minced onion	50 mL
1	clove garlic, minced	1
2 cups	sliced mushrooms (about 4 oz [125 g])	500 mL
1/2 cup	chopped toasted pecans	125 mL
2 tbsp	minced fresh parsley	25 mL
1 tbsp	minced fresh thyme	15 mL
	Salt and pepper to taste	

1. In a saucepan bring 8 cups (2 L) water to a boil. Stir in wheat kernels. Reduce heat to medium-low, cover and cook 1 1/2 hours or until tender. Drain.

2. In a frying pan, melt butter over medium-high heat. Cook onion, garlic and mushrooms for 4 minutes or until tender. Toss with warm wheat, pecans, parsley and thyme. Season to taste with salt and pepper.

SERVES 6

Corn and Squash Fritters

When the Americas were first discovered, central American natives were growing corn, a crop grown by the Mayas more than 2,000 years ago. Early American Indians used corn in their cuisine, too. It has since spread throughout North America and every summer I await the sweet corn grown around the town of Taber, near Lethbridge in southern Alberta.

PREHEAT OVEN TO 225° F (110° C)

1 cup	cooked corn or frozen corn, thawed	250 mL
1/2 cup	low-fat sour cream	125 mL
1/3 cup	all-purpose flour	75 mL
2	eggs	2
1	small zucchini, grated and squeezed to remove excess moisture	1
Half	small onion, minced	Half
1/2 tsp	salt	2 mL
1/4 tsp	black pepper	1 mL
	Canola oil	

1. In a food processor, mince corn. In a bowl stir together corn, sour cream, flour, eggs, zucchini, onion, salt and pepper. Let batter rest 30 minutes.

2. Brush a nonstick skillet with a little canola oil and heat over medium-high heat. Spoon 2 tbsp (25 mL) batter per fritter into hot pan, spreading batter into a 3-inch (8 cm) pancake. Cook for 1 to 2 minutes per side or until golden brown. Hold warm in oven while cooking remaining pancakes. Serve hot.

Fresh Corn Pudding

Try this old-fashioned savory custard when corn is fresh and you're tired of corn on the cob (if that's possible) or use thawed, frozen corn kernels. Serve it as a side dish to roast chicken or meats, or as a light luncheon dish for four, with green salad on the side.

PREHEAT OVEN TO 350° F (180° C)
10-CUP (2.5 L) CASSEROLE DISH OR SOUFFLÉ DISH, GREASED

2 tbsp	butter	25 mL
1	onion, minced	1
1	red bell pepper, chopped	1
1	stalk celery, minced	1
5 cups	fresh corn kernels *or* frozen corn, thawed	1.25 L
2 cups	light (10%) cream *or* evaporated skim milk	500 mL
1/2 tsp	granulated sugar	2 mL
1/2 tsp	salt	2 mL
1/2 tsp	black pepper	2 mL
2	eggs	2
1 tbsp	all-purpose flour	15 mL

1. In a saucepan melt butter over medium heat. Cook onion, red pepper and celery for 10 minutes or until tender. Stir in corn, cream, sugar, salt and pepper. Bring to a boil, reduce heat to medium-low and simmer for 10 minutes. Remove from heat and cool slightly.

2. In a bowl whisk eggs with flour. Beat in a small amount of warm vegetable mixture; stir eggs back into vegetable mixture. Pour into prepared dish. Bake for 40 minutes or until custard is set and top is lightly browned. Let stand 5 minutes before serving.

Walnut and Wild Rice Fritters

These savory little pancakes are great for breakfast with grilled sausage patties, topped with apple butter and smoked turkey. They're also delicious as appetizers — or as a side dish with just about anything! I like to serve them with ROAST DUCKLING WITH WILD BERRIES (see recipe, page 73).

PREHEAT OVEN TO 225° F (110° C)

1/4 cup	butter	50 mL
1/2 cup	chopped onions	125 mL
1/2 cup	all-purpose flour	125 mL
1/2 cup	ground walnuts	125 mL
1 tsp	baking powder	5 mL
1/4 tsp	salt	1 mL
Pinch	white pepper	Pinch
1	egg	1
1/4 cup	yogurt *or* sour cream	50 mL
1/4 cup	milk	50 mL
1 cup	cooked wild rice	250 mL
	Canola oil	

1. In a frying pan, melt butter over medium heat. Add onions and cook for 5 minutes or until tender. Set aside.

2. In a bowl stir together flour, walnuts, baking powder, salt and pepper. In another bowl, whisk together egg, yogurt and milk; stir into dry ingredients just until combined. Let batter stand for 10 minutes.

3. Stir onions and cooked wild rice into batter. Brush a non-stick skillet with a little canola oil and heat over medium heat. Spoon 2 tbsp (25 mL) batter per fritter into hot pan, spreading batter into a 3-inch (7.5 cm) pancake. Cook for 2 minutes per side or until golden brown. Hold warm in oven while cooking remaining pancakes. Serve hot.

Baked Cowboy Rice

This warming rice dish provides a wonderful balance of spicy salsa, sweet corn and savory cheese.

PREHEAT OVEN TO 350° F (180° C)
13- BY 9-INCH (3 L) BAKING DISH

3 cups	long grain brown rice	750 mL
2 cups	low-fat sour cream	500 mL
3 cups	medium salsa	750 mL
2 cups	shredded old Cheddar cheese	500 mL
2 cups	shredded Monterey Jack cheese	500 mL
2 cups	frozen corn, thawed	500 mL

1. In a saucepan bring 4 cups (1 L) of water to a boil. Add rice, return to boil, cover, reduce heat to low and cook for 20 minutes. Do not uncover. Remove pan from heat and let stand 10 minutes. Cool.

2. In a large bowl, combine cooled rice, sour cream, 2 cups (500 mL) of the salsa, 1 1/2 cups (375 mL) of the Cheddar, 1 1/2 cups (375 mL) of the Monterey Jack and 1 1/2 cups (375 mL) of the corn. Mix well and turn into baking dish. Spoon remaining cheeses, salsa and corn down the center of the dish, forming four separate lines.

3. Bake, uncovered, for 30 minutes or until heated through.

Wild Rice Casserole with Oyster Mushrooms and Toasted Almonds

SERVES 6

Low in fat and high in protein and Vitamin B, wild rice has a nutty flavor and chewy texture.

Early French explorers were probably the first non-natives to enjoy wild rice. In historical documents, they describe the great wars fought by the Ojibway and Sioux over this precious food. Eighteenth century explorer Alexander Henry wrote that without wild rice, travel west beyond the Saskatchewan River would have been impossible.

PREHEAT OVEN TO 350° F (180° C)
6-CUP (1.5 L) CASSEROLE DISH WITH LID

2 tbsp	butter	25 mL
1	onion, finely chopped	1
1	clove garlic, minced	1
1 cup	sliced oyster mushrooms	250 mL
1/2 cup	minced celery	125 mL
1 cup	wild rice	250 mL
1 cup	slivered toasted almonds	250 mL
3 cups	chicken stock	750 mL
	Salt and pepper to taste	

1. In a saucepan melt butter over medium heat; cook onion, garlic, mushrooms and celery 5 minutes or until tender. Stir in wild rice and almonds; cook 3 minutes or until nuts begin to brown. In a separate saucepan, bring chicken stock to a boil.

2. Put rice mixture in casserole dish; pour hot chicken stock over it. Cover and bake for one hour or until rice is tender. Season to taste with salt and pepper.

arly cowboys ate beef and beans for breakfast. But now it's the pancake or flapjack that starts a cowboy's day in the West. The pancake breakfast is as synonymous with Calgary and the annual Stampede as cowboys and beef. Every July, you'll see these massive free feeds of flapjacks, sausages and strong coffee spring up like mushrooms in mall parking lots, community centers and backyard decks. Big breakfasts have been a western tradition ever since cowboys on the range perched on their bedrolls to eat bacon and beans before dawn. And everyone baked in the Old West — farm wives challenged temperamental wood stoves and range cooks baked bread and biscuits in campfire Dutch ovens. The first settlers used sourdough starters or baking powder to raise their breads before active dry yeast was available, making flat or fry breads the first popular breads on early Western tables. Bread was an integral part of the pioneer diet and range cooks baked their bread in Dutch ovens. These heavy cast-iron pots came complete with heavy concave lids and stilt-like feet so they could stand right in the middle of a bed of hot coals. When the bread dough was formed into loaves, it was placed in the greased and preheated Dutch oven, then covered with the lid. Several hot coals were then positioned around the top of the lid, creating a little oven inside the pan. A batch of biscuits will bake this way in 15 minutes. I've seen cowboys cook entire roasts and round loaves of peasant bread in these ingenious campfire ovens, and you'll still find modern versions for sale at local camping supply stores. There is a definite etiquette about checking the food or removing anything from these charcoal-covered ovens — use a heavy oven mitt or pot hook to remove the lid, opening it away from you so the steam goes away from the cook. And be careful that the ashes don't fall into the food, a serious cowboy cuisine faux pas.

Cowboy Flapjacks, Biscuits & Baking

MAKES ABOUT
18 PANCAKES

Buttermilk Flapjacks

Cowboys in the Old West couldn't count on having maple syrup on the table for their morning pancakes. Many just slopped on some "Charlie Taylor" — a sweet mixture of bacon grease and molasses that took the place of syrup.

5 cups	all-purpose flour	1.25 L
3 tbsp	granulated sugar	45 mL
2 tsp	baking soda	10 mL
1 tsp	baking powder	5 mL
3 cups	buttermilk	750 mL
2 cups	half-and-half cream	500 mL
5	eggs, beaten	5
1/4 cup	melted butter	50 mL
1 tsp	vanilla	5 mL

1. In a large mixing bowl, stir together flour, sugar, baking soda and baking powder.

2. In a measuring cup, whisk together buttermilk, half-and-half, eggs, butter and vanilla. Stir into flour to make a smooth batter.

3. Spoon batter onto a hot, greased griddle or seasoned cast iron pan and cook until bubbles form on one side. Flip the pancakes and brown the second side. Serve immediately.

Cornmeal and Berry Pancakes

These cornmeal pancakes are crisp and flavorful, like cornbread shot with prairie berries.

If you can't find Saskatoon berries, substitute fresh or frozen blueberries or even raspberries in these delectable hotcakes.

1/2 cup	cornmeal	125 mL
1/2 cup	boiling water	125 mL
1/2 cup	all-purpose flour	125 mL
1 tbsp	baking powder	15 mL
1 tbsp	granulated sugar	15 mL
1/2 tsp	salt	2 mL
1	egg	1
1/4 cup	melted butter	50 mL
1/4 cup	milk	50 mL
1 cup	fresh Saskatoon berries *or* fresh or frozen blueberries	250 mL

1. In a large bowl, combine cornmeal and boiling water; stir well. Set aside.

2. In a mixing bowl, stir together flour, salt, sugar and baking powder.

3. In another bowl, whisk together egg with melted butter and milk.

4. Add dry and wet ingredients to cornmeal and stir until blended. Fold berries into pancakes (If you're using frozen berries, don't thaw them.)

5. Heat a nonstick pan over medium-high heat and brush with a little oil. Reduce heat to medium and spoon about 1/4 cup (50 mL) batter into pan, spreading with the back of a spoon if necessary to form 3-inch (7.5 cm) cakes.

6. Cook until bubbles break on top, 1 to 2 minutes, then turn over and cook second side until golden. Serve hot with maple syrup.

MAKES 18 TO 24 PANCAKES

Fruit-Filled Flapjacks

When cowboys call their pancakes "splatter dabs" or "wheelers" they couldn't be referring to these tender buttermilk cakes filled with healthy grains and fresh fruit.

1/2 cup	all-purpose flour	125 mL
1/4 cup	wheat germ	50 mL
1 tsp	baking powder	5 mL
1/2 tsp	baking soda	2 mL
Pinch	salt	Pinch
1 cup	buttermilk *or* yogurt	250 mL
2 tbsp	canola oil	25 mL
1 tbsp	sugar	15 mL
2	eggs	2
1/2 to 1 cup	fresh fruit (grated apple, sliced peaches, bananas, strawberries or blueberries	125 to 250 mL

1. In a mixing bowl, stir together flour, wheat germ, baking powder, baking soda and salt.
2. In a measuring cup, whisk together buttermilk, oil, sugar and eggs.
3. Stir liquid ingredients into dry ingredients just to moisten. Gently stir in fruit.
4. Cook pancakes on a hot, greased skillet. Wait until bubbles break on top of cakes and edges begin to brown, then flip and brown second side. Serve immediately with yogurt, honey and maple syrup.

MAKES 8 TO 10 SERVINGS

Cree Bannock with Currants

This rich, biscuit-like bread entered the Native diet after the first fur traders arrived with flour. Originally a Scottish recipe, bannock quickly became a staple food on the prairies.

PREHEAT OVEN TO 375° F (190° C)

6 cups	all-purpose flour	1.5 L
3 tbsp	baking powder	45 mL
1 tbsp	salt	15 mL
1 1/2 cups	lard *or* vegetable shortening	375 mL
2 cups	currants	500 mL
3 cups	water	750 mL

1. In a large mixing bowl, stir together flour, baking powder and salt. Add lard and, with your fingers or a pastry cutter, work in to flour mixture to form coarse crumbs. Stir in currants.

2. Add enough water to make a soft dough; and divide dough between two 8-inch (2 L) round pans.

3. Bake in preheated oven 30 to 40 minutes or until a toothpick inserted in center comes out clean. Cut into wedges. Serve with butter and berry jam.

Oatmeal and Molasses Bread

I collected this recipe several years ago from old-time rancher Albert Maynard, who cooked it campfire-style in a cowboy Dutch oven. This is an ingenious process: typically, about 10 hot coals are positioned under the oven, with 7 or 8 on the lid. If the dish requires more than an hour of baking time, more coals are added —both under and on top of the pot. I've never baked this way myself, but this old cowboy obviously had lots of practice because his bread was cooked to perfection.

Albert's recipe makes a rich, dark loaf that's delicious for breakfast, even if your oven's electric.

PREHEAT OVEN TO 375° F (190° C)
PIE PANS, GREASED

2	packages traditional yeast	2
1 tsp	granulated sugar	5 mL
1 cup	warm water	250 mL
2 cups	quick oats	500 mL
1/2 cup	Alberta honey or other honey	125 mL
1/2 cup	molasses	125 mL
1 tsp	salt	5 mL
2 tbsp	vegetable oil	25 mL
4 cups	boiling water	1 L
9 to 10 cups	all-purpose flour (about 3 lbs [1.5 kg])	2.2 L to 2.5 L

1. In a mixing bowl, sprinkle yeast and sugar over warm water and set aside for 10 minutes.

2. In a large mixing bowl, stir together oats, molasses, honey, salt and vegetable oil with boiling water. Add dissolved yeast and gradually beat in flour, mixing well to form a smooth soft dough.

3. Divide dough into 3 parts and shape each into a round loaf. Place loaves in greased pie pans and let rise in a warm place, covered with a towel, until doubled in bulk (about 1 1/2 hours).

4. Bake in preheated oven for 35 to 45 minutes, or until loaves sound hollow when tapped on the bottom. Serve with berry jam.

Dill Beer Bread

Beer is a natural beverage in the West — created with the barley that is one of our major cash crops.

Over 100 years ago, Albert Ernest (A.E.) Cross, one of Calgary's early beef and business tycoons, formed the Calgary Brewing & Malting Co., supplying beer to his own chain of hotels. For many years, his Calgary beer, with it's big buffalo on the label, was the beer of choice in Cowtown.

Today brew pubs and microbreweries are introducing a new generation to pure, naturally-brewed beer made with those simple ingredients — barley, yeast, hops and water. The grand daddy of the microbreweries in Western Canada is Calgary's Big Rock Brewery, producing world-famous brews like Big Rock Traditional and Grasshopper ales.

PREHEAT OVEN TO 350° F (180° C)
8- BY 4-INCH (1.5 L) LOAF PAN

3 cups	all-purpose flour	750 mL
1 tbsp + 1 tsp	baking powder	15 mL + 5 mL
3 tbsp	brown sugar	45 mL
2 tbsp	fresh dill	25 mL
1 1/2 tsp	salt	7 mL
1/2 tsp	baking soda	2 mL
1	bottle (12 oz [341 mL]) beer (Big Rock Traditional Ale is a good choice) or favorite ale	1
1	egg	1

1. In a food processor, combine flour, baking powder, sugar, dill, salt and baking soda. Pulse 2 seconds just to mix. Add half the beer and pulse 4 times. Add the remaining beer and pulse until just blended. Do not overmix.

2. Pour batter into prepared loaf pan. Bake in preheated oven for about 45 minutes or until a toothpick inserted in center comes out clean. Let cool on rack for 10 minutes. Serve warm.

Spicy Cowboy Corn Bread

*Cornmeal is a popular
ingredient in
Western cooking, where
it finds its way into
pancakes and breads, or
is simply eaten hot with
milk, butter and syrup.
Served with meat and
gravy, it can replace
potatoes. In the early
days, cornmeal was also
the basis for Indian
Pudding, a favorite
dessert at that time.*

PREHEAT OVEN TO 400° F (200° C)
9-INCH SQUARE (2.5 L) BAKING PAN OR MUFFIN TINS, GREASED

1 cup	cornmeal	250 mL
1/2 cup	all-purpose flour	125 mL
1 tsp	baking powder	5 mL
1/2 tsp	baking soda	2 mL
1/2 tsp	salt	2 mL
3	eggs	3
3/4 cup	skim milk	175 mL
1/4 cup	canola oil	50 mL
1 cup	corn kernels	250 mL
1/2 cup	grated old Cheddar	125 mL
1/2 cup	minced jalapeno peppers	125 mL

1. In a mixing bowl, stir together cornmeal, flour, baking powder, soda and salt.

2. In another bowl, whisk together eggs with milk and oil. Stir in corn, cheese and peppers. Quickly mix this into the dry ingredients. Be careful that you don't overmix.

3. Pour batter into prepared baking pan or muffin tins. Bake in preheated oven for about 25 minutes or until firm to the touch. Cool on a wire rack and cut into squares.

MAKES 9 LARGE MUFFINS

Beer and Cheddar Muffins

Serve these savory muffins with a black bean and pork chili. Try to find a local cheese, like the aged cheddar from Neapolis Dairy in Didsbury, Alberta.

PREHEAT OVEN TO 400° F (200° C)

MUFFIN TINS, GREASED

2 cups	all-purpose flour	500 mL
2 tbsp	granulated sugar	25 mL
1 tsp	baking powder	5 mL
1/2 tsp	dry mustard	2 mL
1/2 tsp	salt	2 mL
1 cup	beer	250 mL
1/4 cup	canola oil	50 mL
1	egg	1
1 1/4 cups	grated old Cheddar cheese	300 mL

1. In a medium bowl, stir together flour, sugar, baking powder, mustard and salt.

2. In another bowl, whisk together the beer, oil and egg. Mix in the cheese. Add to flour mixture; stir until just combined. Do not overmix.

3. Spoon batter into muffin tins and bake in preheated oven for about 20 to 25 minutes or until golden brown and firm to the touch.

MAKES 8 TO 10

Fluffy Baking Powder Biscuits

Cowboy cooks made biscuits on the range right in the flour sack: they made a well in the flour and stirred into it a little soda and bacon grease, then added enough river water to make a stiff dough. The biscuits were hand-formed and cooked in a frying pan or cast iron Dutch oven over the campfire. It's no wonder these cowboy staples got a bad name — they often had the consistency of hockey pucks, earning them names like "paperweights", "sinkers" or "belly busters."

Tradition notwithstanding, you want your biscuits to be light and flaky. The trick to perfect biscuits is to handle the dough as little as possible. Mix and roll these quickly and they'll stay light and fluffy.

PREHEAT OVEN TO 450° F (230° C)
BAKING SHEET

2 cups	all-purpose flour	500 mL
1 tbsp	baking powder	15 mL
1 tsp	sugar	5 mL
1/2 tsp	salt	2 mL
1/3 cup	butter	75 mL
3/4 cup	half-and-half or light cream	175 mL

1. In a mixing bowl, stir together flour, baking powder, sugar and salt. Cut in butter with a pastry blender to form coarse crumbs. Stir in half-and-half just until moistened. (Do not add extra flour to dough for kneading, since it will already be dry.)

2. Gather dough into a ball and knead gently. (Do not overwork or biscuits will be tough.) Pat dough flat to a 3/4-inch (15 mm) thickness and, using a cutter or a floured glass, cut out 8 to 10 circles, about 2 1/2 inches (6 cm) in diameter.

3. Arrange biscuits 1 inch (2.5 cm) apart on baking sheet. Bake in preheated oven until golden, about 12 to 15 minutes. Serve warm with butter and crabapple jelly or use in your favorite shortcake recipe.

*Egg wash — the egg
and milk mixture
used to coat baked foods
— adds a golden sheen
and acts as glue to
make seeds or grains
stick to the surface.*

*A glass may be used as
a cutter*

Whole Wheat Biscuits

PREHEAT OVEN TO 425° F (220° C)

BAKING SHEET

2 cups	whole wheat flour	500 mL
2 cups	all-purpose flour	500 mL
3 tbsp	baking powder	45 mL
1/2 tsp	salt	2 mL
1/2 cup	vegetable shortening	125 mL
1/2 cup	butter	125 mL
1 1/2 cups	milk	375 mL
1	egg	1
2 tbsp	milk	25 mL
1 tbsp	poppy seeds	15 mL

1. Combine whole wheat flour, all-purpose flour, baking powder and salt. Cut shortening and butter into flour mixture using a pastry blender or 2 knives, until mixture resembles coarse crumbs. Stir in the milk with a fork until just moistened.

2. Turn onto a floured board and knead gently 12 times. Roll or pat gently to 1/2-inch (1 cm) thickness and cut into biscuits using a 3-inch (7.5 cm) cutter.

3. In a small bowl, whisk together egg and milk. Brush biscuits with egg wash; dip tops into bowl containing the poppy seeds.

4. Place biscuits on baking sheet and bake in preheated oven for 25 minutes or until golden brown.

Smoky Red Pepper and Cheese Scones

These big biscuits, filled with smoky roasted peppers and hearty cheddar cheese are very large, making a portable meal in themselves.

PREHEAT OVEN TO 350° F (180° C)
2 BAKING SHEETS LINED WITH PARCHMENT PAPER

3	roasted red bell peppers	3
6 cups	all-purpose flour	1.5 L
2 tbsp	granulated sugar	25 mL
1 1/2 tbsp	baking powder	20 mL
2 tbsp	chopped fresh basil	25 mL
2 tbsp	chopped parsley	25 mL
1 tsp	freshly ground black pepper	5 mL
1/2 tsp	salt	2 mL
2/3 cup	butter, softened	150 mL
2 cups	buttermilk	500 mL
3	large eggs	3
8 oz	old Cheddar or smoked gouda cheese, cut into small cubes	250 g

1. Use well drained, roasted peppers from a jar or roast bell peppers from scratch. To roast, grill peppers on barbecue or under broiler until blackened on all sides. Place in a paper bag to steam and cool for 10 minutes, then remove skin, seeds and ribs. Chop roasted peppers.

2. In a large bowl, combine flour, sugar, baking powder chopped herbs, salt and pepper. Cut butter into cubes and work butter into flour mixture to form coarse crumbs.

3. In a separate bowl, beat eggs with buttermilk and mix with dry ingredients until barely combined. Fold in roasted peppers and cheese. Do not overmix.

4. Scoop about 3/4 cup (175 mL) of batter onto prepared baking sheets (5 large scones per sheet), leaving 2 inches (5 cm) between scones for expansion. Flatten slightly. Bake in preheated oven for 30 to 35 minutes or until scones are golden and tops spring back to the touch.

Orange Scones with CPR Strawberries

very early cowboy survived on biscuits. Scones are simply sweet biscuits, gussied up with fruit and other tasty additions. When real strawberries were few and far between on the prairies, the only fruit that came West on the train was the portable prune, which cowboys called "CPR strawberries."

PREHEAT OVEN TO 400° F (200° C)

BAKING SHEET

3 cups	all-purpose flour	750 mL
1/2 cup	granulated sugar	125 mL
4 tsp	baking powder	20 mL
1/2 tsp	salt	2 mL
1/2 cup	butter	125 mL
1	egg	1
1 cup	buttermilk	250 mL
1 cup	pitted prunes, chopped (about 4 oz [125])	250 mL
2 tsp	grated orange zest	10 mL
	Egg wash (1 egg beaten with 2 tbsp [25 mL] milk)	

1. In a large bowl, mix flour, sugar, baking powder and salt. Using a pastry blender, cut in the butter until the mixture resembles coarse crumbs.

2. In a separate bowl, beat egg with buttermilk; stir into flour mixture with chopped prunes and orange peel. Mix well.

3. Turn dough out onto a lightly floured surface and knead gently, 5 or 6 times, or until smooth.

4. Divide dough into 16 balls. Flatten into disks, 1/2-inch (1 cm) thick. Place scones on baking sheet, brush with egg wash and bake in preheated oven for about 20 minutes or until golden. Serve warm or at room temperature.

Pumpkin Date Nut Muffins

Scissors work well cutting sticky fruit like prunes and dates.

Be sure to use pumpkin purée — not pumpkin pie filling, which contains a lot of added seasonings.

PREHEAT OVEN TO 400° F (200° C)
MUFFIN TINS, WELL GREASED

2 cups	all-purpose flour	500 mL
1 tsp	baking powder	5 mL
1 tsp	baking soda	5 mL
1 tsp	cinnamon	5 mL
1/2 tsp	ground cloves	2 mL
1/2 tsp	salt	2 mL
2 cups	canned pumpkin purée	250 mL
1/2 cup	butter *or* margarine	125 mL
1 1/2 cups	granulated sugar	375 mL
3	eggs	3
2/3 cup	water	150 mL
3/4 cup	chopped dates	175 mL
3/4 cup	chopped pecans	175 mL

1. In a mixing bowl, combine flour, baking powder, baking soda, cinnamon, cloves and salt.

2. In a separate bowl, cream butter and sugar until fluffy. Add eggs and beat thoroughly. Stir in pumpkin purée and water and beat well. Pour over dry ingredients; stir together just until moistened. Fold in the dates and nuts.

3. Spoon batter into muffin tins almost three-quarters full and bake in preheated for 20 to 30 minutes or until firm to the touch. Cool on racks.

BUTTERMILK FLAPJACKS (PAGE 148) ➤

Almond Stollen with Currants, Raisins and Apricots

MAKES 1 LOAF

I received this recipe several years ago from Kathy Bossart, the creative baker at Caribou Lodge, a mountain destination for heli-hikers and skiers. It's very moist but substantial — good for the backpack when you're off on a hike in the mountains, or pretty on a plate for an elegant brunch.

Dried fruit has always been a staple on the prairies where fresh fruit was not always available and this sweet bread reflects the German settlers who came early to the West.

2 1/2 cups	all-purpose flour	625 mL
3/4 cup	ground almonds	175 mL
1 tbsp	baking powder	15 mL
3/4 cup	granulated sugar	175 mL
1/2 tsp	salt	2 mL
1/4 tsp	mace	1 mL
1/8 tsp	cardamom *or* a mixture of allspice and cinnamon	0.5 mL
1/2 cup	cold butter	125 mL
1 cup	cottage cheese *or* sour cream	250 mL
1	egg	1
2 tbsp	rum	25 mL
1/2 tsp	vanilla	2 mL
1/4 tsp	almond extract	1 mL
1/2 cup	currants	125 mL
1/2 cup	golden raisins	125 mL
1/2 cup	chopped dried apricots	125 mL

1. In a mixing bowl, combine the flour, almonds, baking powder, sugar, salt, mace and cardamom; cut in butter until mixture resembles coarse crumbs.

2. Using a food processor, purée cottage cheese, egg, rum, vanilla and almond extract until smooth. Fold into flour mixture, along with currants, raisins and apricots. Form dough into a ball and knead on a floured surface until smooth and elastic.

3. On a piece of parchment, roll dough into an 8- by 10-inch (20 by 25 cm) rectangle and transfer to baking sheet. Crease dough slightly off-center parallel to long side. Brush dough with melted butter and using parchment paper, fold smaller section over larger one. Bake at 350° F (180° C) for 50 to 60 minutes, until dark golden brown. Remove from oven and brush top with melted butter and sprinkle with sugar. Store loaf in an airtight container for 2 to 3 days to mellow.

◄ WILD BERRY SHORTCAKE (PAGE 169) WITH COWBOY COFFEE (PAGE 184)

Grandma's Poppyseed Roll

When I was a kid, my Serbian grand-mother used to make us this wonderful roll — heavy and dense with lots of dark poppy seed filling.

3	packages traditional yeast	3
3 tsp	sugar	15 mL
1 1/2 cups	lukewarm water	375 mL
2 cups	milk, scalded and cooled	250 mL
3	eggs, beaten	3
1 1/2 cups	granulated sugar	375 L
3/4 cup	butter *or* lard	175 mL
1 tsp	salt	5 mL
10 to 12 cups	all-purpose flour	2.5 to 3 L

Filling

2 cups	poppy seeds, ground in a food processor (my Grandma used an old manual coffee grinder for this)	500 mL
2 cups	milk	500 mL
1 cup	granulated sugar	250 mL
2	eggs, beaten	2
	Juice of 1 lemon	
1/2 cup	butter, softened	125 mL

1. In a mixing bowl, sprinkle yeast and sugar over water. Let stand 10 minutes.

2. In another bowl, combine milk, eggs, sugar, butter and salt. Beat in yeast mixture and enough flour to make a soft dough. Set dough in a greased bowl, cover and set aside in a warm place to rise for about 1 1/2 hours or until doubled. Punch down dough and let rise a second time.

3. Meanwhile, make the filling: In a saucepan, combine poppy seeds, milk and sugar; bring to a boil. Cook for 10 minutes; remove from heat. Add beaten eggs and lemon juice. Return to heat and cook, stirring, until thick and spreadable.

To scald milk, heat milk in a saucepan until bubbles begin to form around the edge of the pan. The milk does not boil.

A coffee grinder does a great job of grinding poppyseeds.

Some bulk stores carry ground poppyseeds.

Egg wash is egg beaten with 2 tbsp (25 mL) milk or water to give a golden sheen to baking.

4. Divide dough into 6 equal portions and roll each into a large rectangle, about 13 by 10 inches (32.5 by 25 cm). Spread entire dough with butter, then spread with about 1/3 cup (75 mL) filling. Roll up like a jelly roll and place seam side down on baking sheet. Cover with a tea towel and let rise another 30 minutes.

5. Brush with egg wash and bake at 375° F (190° C) for 30 minutes or until golden brown and firm to the touch. Cool on racks. Slice to serve. These rolls freeze well.

There may have been little in the way of fresh fruit in the Old West, but even cowboys feasted on pie. ⚘ On the farm, apples could be kept in cold storage much of the winter and in the summer, there were wild berries — including strawberries, gooseberries and saskatoons — to use in pies. ⚘ Prairie staples included dried prunes and apples, dates and raisins, so pies and tarts also contained these goodies. The basic pastry was made with flour and lard, rendered from animals after butchering, and there was usually a good supply of fresh cream, milk and butter on the ranch. Chuck wagon cooks bought flour and sugar by the barrel, the latter often needed to be put through a sugar grinder to pulverize the lumps before it could be used. ⚘ Chuckwagon cooks also specialized in pies and puddings using wild fruit and dried staples, although dessert was a rare treat on the trail. Cookie baked his pies, like his breads, in a Dutch oven over the embers of a campfire, using lard in the crust or biscuit dough to encase fillings of raisins and currants or stewed prunes. ⚘ Some cowboy cooks made vinegar pies — filled with a kind of sweet-and-sour custard made with vinegar, water, fat, flour and sugar, then baked with a lattice top. ⚘ Pies were often eaten out of the hand, so cowboy cooks made sturdy pastry, sometimes creating fruit turnovers or "fried pies", half moons of filled pastry browned in deep fat. ⚘ Steamed puddings were especially popular on early Western tables in Canada, a result of many early cowboys' British roots. But all cowboy cooks from San Antonio to Dodge City created steamed puddings with dried fruit, the most famous version being the colorfully-named "son-of-a-bitch-in-a-sack." This pudding — of flour, suet and fruit — was steamed in a flour sack, then boiled for several hours and served with a sweet sauce. ⚘ Try these updated versions of pies, puddings and cakes using old-fashioned and indigenous ingredients, from rhubarb and saskatoons to dried fruits and storable vegetables like carrots.

Pies, Cakes & Old-Fashioned Desserts

Cranberry Rhubarb Pot Pie

Rhubarb grows like a weed in Western Canada. It's the first thing up in the garden and this perennial grows back no matter how harsh the winter. Rhubarb is tart and mouth-puckering when raw but we used to eat it as kids, dipped in sugar. It's so good alone or with strawberries in pie, rhubarb has won the nickname The Pie Plant. But don't eat the leaves, they're poisonous.

This easy pot pie recipe comes from the chefs at Deer Lodge in Lake Louise.

PREHEAT OVEN TO 400° F (200° C)
DEEP PIE PLATE (8-INCH [2 L])
   OR SHALLOW ROUND CASSEROLE DISH

Filling

2 cups	granulated sugar	500 mL
3 cups	cranberries (fresh or frozen), chopped	750 mL
2 cups	rhubarb (fresh or frozen)	500 mL
1 cup	fresh orange juice	250 mL
1	vanilla bean *or* 1 tsp (5 mL) vanilla extract	1
1	cinnamon stick	1
1 tsp	fresh black pepper	5 mL
1- to 2-inch	piece ginger root, peeled	2 to 5 cm

Biscuit dough

2 cups	all-purpose flour	500 mL
1 tsp	baking powder	5 mL
1/2 tsp	salt	2 mL
1/4 cup	granulated sugar	50 mL
1/2 cup	cold butter	125 mL
3/4 cup	buttermilk	175 mL

1. In a heavy frying pan over low heat, heat sugar for about 15 minutes or until it's dark and caramel colored. The sugar will melt as it heats; you can add 1 tbsp (15 mL) of water to speed up the process. Keep a close watch so it doesn't burn.

2. Very carefully add the cranberries, rhubarb and orange juice to the hot caramelized sugar. (It will steam and sputter.) Cook over medium heat until sugar is dissolved completely. Add the vanilla bean, cinnamon stick, pepper and ginger; simmer until entire mixture is reduced to a thick, jam-like consistency, about 10 minutes.

Bake pot pie with a cookie sheet or piece of foil underneath to catch any drips.

3. Remove vanilla bean, cinnamon stick and ginger root, and place filling in a deep pie plate.

4. For biscuit topping: in a mixing bowl, combine flour, baking powder, salt and sugar and cut in butter with a pastry blender until mixture resembles coarse crumbs. Add buttermilk and mix just until dough forms a ball. Turn out on a lightly floured surface and pat into a uniformly-thick circle, big enough to cover your pie plate.

5. Cover pie with biscuit dough and crimp edges decoratively. Brush dough with mixture of 1 egg beaten with 2 tbsp (25 mL) milk or water and sprinkle with granulated sugar. Bake in preheated oven until golden and bubbly, about 20 to 30 minutes. Serve with ice cream or vanilla yogurt.

SERVES 6

Upside Down Apple Gingerbread

When it came to finding fuel for heating, cooking and baking, early prairie settlers had to make do with what was at hand. With no trees in sight, they burned dried cow chips (manure). Farm women and children would gather manure chips up to a mile away from their homestead, and stack them like small haystacks near the house. Cow chips were also known as "prairie coal."

PREHEAT OVEN TO 350° F (180° C)
9-INCH (23 CM) ROUND CAKE PAN

1 2/3 cups	granulated sugar	400 mL
1/3 cup	water	75 mL
2	apples, peeled, cored and sliced	2
1 2/3 cups	all-purpose flour	400 mL
1 1/2 tsp	ground ginger	7 mL
1 tsp	baking soda	5 mL
1 tbsp	cinnamon	15 mL
1/4 tsp	ground cloves	1 mL
1/4 tsp	salt	1 mL
1/2 cup	shortening	125 mL
1	egg	1
3/4 cups	buttermilk	175 mL
2 tbsp	molasses	25 mL

1. In a heavy saucepan, stir together 2/3 cup (150 mL) of sugar and water; bring to a boil. Reduce heat to medium and cook for 5 to 10 minutes or until deep amber in color. Pour into cake pan and arrange sliced apples over bottom of pan, overlapping to form a neat pattern.

2. In a large bowl, stir together flour, remaining sugar, ginger, baking soda, cinnamon, cloves and salt. Cut in shortening until mixture resembles coarse crumbs.

3. In a small bowl, beat egg with buttermilk and molasses; stir into dry mixture. Pour batter over apples in pan and bake in preheated oven for 50 to 60 minutes or until firm to the touch. Cool slightly on rack.

4. Run a knife around edge of cooled cake and invert onto serving platter. Cut into wedges and serve with whipped cream or ice cream.

SERVES 6

Wild Berry Shortcake

ild berries include wild strawberries and raspberries, as well as low-bush and high-bush cranberries, chokecherries, Nanking cherries and wild currants. These have been used by natives, settlers and current prairie residents for hundreds of years. Find your own favorite patch or look for these wild delicacies at summer farmer's markets.

PREHEAT OVEN TO 425° F (220° C)

BAKING SHEET

2 lbs	fresh berries (mixture of blueberries, wild strawberries, saskatoons, raspberries, etc.), about 8 cups (2 L)	1 kg
1/4 cup	apple juice *or* berry liqueur	50 mL
1/4 cup	granulated sugar	50 mL

Biscuit

1/2 cup	all purpose flour	125 mL
1/2 cup	whole wheat flour	125 mL
1/4 cup	ground pecans *or* walnuts	50 mL
1/2 cup	brown sugar	125 mL
1/2 tsp	salt	2 mL
2 tsp	baking powder	10 mL
1 tsp	baking soda	5 mL
1/4 cup	butter	50 mL
1/2 cup	yogurt	125 mL
1/2 tsp	vanilla	2 mL
1 cup	whipping (35%) cream, whipped with a little sugar *or* 1 cup [250 mL] low-fat vanilla yogurt)	250 mL

1. In a bowl combine fruit with juice and sugar; let stand.

2. Meanwhile, in another bowl, stir together flours, pecans, brown sugar, salt, baking powder and baking soda. Cut in butter with a pastry cutter to form coarse crumbs. Stir in yogurt and vanilla just to combine.

3. Place biscuit dough on a slightly floured surface and pat to a 1-inch (2.5 cm) thickness. Cut into 2-inch (5 cm) circles with a biscuit cutter, brush with some milk and sprinkle with granulated sugar. Bake in preheated oven until golden, about 10 to 15 minutes. Cool slightly.

4. Cut biscuits in half horizontally and place bottom half on dessert plate. Top with some of the berry mixture, some whipped cream or yogurt, the second half of the biscuit then more berries and cream.

SERVES 8 TO 10

Berry Bread Pudding with Maple Brandy Sauce

Wild or U-pick, berries abound in the West during the summer months. In Alberta, for U-pick strawberries, saskatoons, raspberries and other fresh produce, contact the Alberta Market Gardeners Association at 1-800-661-2642. They also publish an annual Come to Our Farm guide, with addresses of 150 U-pick farms and market gardens across the province.

PREHEAT OVEN TO 325° F (160° C)
13- BY 9-INCH (3 L) BAKING PAN, BUTTERED

Custard

4 cups	2 % milk	1 L
1 cup	granulated sugar	250 mL
6	eggs	6
3	egg yolks	3
1 tbsp	vanilla	15 mL
2 tsp	cinnamon	10 mL
8 cups	bread cubes, 3/4-inch (15 mm) pieces from day old bread	2 L
1 lb	saskatoons or blueberries, fresh or frozen (thawed and well-drained)	500 g
1 tbsp	minced orange zest	15 mL
	Confectioner's sugar for dusting	

Maple Brandy Sauce

1 1/2 cups	half-and-half cream	375 mL
1/8 tsp	vanilla extract	0.5 mL
2 tbsp	sugar	25 mL
2	egg yolks	2
1/8 tsp	salt	0.5 mL
1/4 cup	maple syrup	125 mL
2 tbsp	brandy *or* Grand Marnier	25 mL

1. In heavy saucepan over medium-high heat, whisk together milk, sugar, eggs, yolks, vanilla and cinnamon. Whisk constantly for about 10 minutes or until custard is just starting to thicken. Remove from heat.

2. Place half the bread cubes in prepared baking pan. Sprinkle with half the saskatoons or blueberries, and half of the orange zest. Repeat layers.

For a richer pudding, use 2 cups (500 mL) of whipping cream to replace half of the milk in the custard.

3. Pour the custard over top and gently press down, allowing the bread to soak for at least 4 hours or overnight (cover pan with plastic and soak in refrigerator). If all custard cannot be added initially, it can be added after sitting in the refrigerator.

4. Bake in preheated oven for 60 to 70 minutes or until a toothpick inserted in the center comes out almost dry. After baking, allow pudding to cool for at least 15 minutes to set up before cutting. You may also make the pudding in advance, cool and reheat in the microwave before serving.

5. For sauce, in heavy saucepan, heat half-and-half and vanilla until bubbles appear around the edge. Whisk sugar, egg yolks and salt together until light. Slowly whisk some of the hot cream into the egg mixture, then whisk all back into the pot. Cook the sauce over medium-low heat until it thickens. Cool to room temperature, then stir in maple syrup and brandy or Grand Marnier.

6. To serve, cut warm pudding into squares and set in individual deep dishes, in a pool of sauce. Dust with icing sugar.

Carrot Figgy Pudding with Caramel Cream

During the long cold winters, prairie cooks often had little to work with apart from carrots and other root vegetables stored in their cellars and cold rooms.

Real cowboys scoffed at drinking milk, but there was always a little red can of Carnation in the pantry — affectionately dubbed "tin cow" — for baking or adding to your coffee.

Steamed carrot pudding is a Christmas tradition at my husband's home in rural Alberta. His mother, Joan Meeres, makes a wonderful rich pudding, filled with carrots and spices. Here is a version of that old-fashioned winter dessert, with a caramel sauce inspired by the "cajeta," made with goat's milk in Mexican cooking.

1/2 cup	chopped butter *or* lard	125 mL
1 cup	dark brown sugar	250 mL
1 cup	grated carrots	250 mL
1 cup	grated apples	250 mL
3/4 cup	all-purpose flour	175 mL
1 tsp	baking soda	5 mL
1/2 tsp	cinnamon	2 mL
1/2 tsp	ground cloves	2 mL
1/4 tsp	ground nutmeg	1 mL
1 cup	raisins	250 mL
1 cup	chopped figs *or* dried currants	250 mL

Caramel Cream

1	can (14 oz [398 mL]) evaporated milk	1
1	can (12 oz [300 mL]) sweetened condensed milk	1
2 tbsp	unsalted butter	25 mL

1. In a mixing bowl using an electric mixer, beat the butter and brown sugar until fluffy. Add grated carrots and apples.
2. Sift the flour, baking soda and nutmeg, cloves and cinnamon over the raisins and currants or figs. Mix well and stir into the carrot mixture.
3. Turn into a greased 6-cup (1.5 L) pudding mold or heat-proof bowl, making sure there is enough room for the pudding to expand. Cover the bowl with a piece of greased wax paper and a layer of foil, tied around the rim with a string.
4. Place the pudding on a rack in large pot or canning kettle and fill it with hot water, coming halfway up the sides of the mold. Cover pot, bring water to a boil, reduce heat and steam pudding for 2 hours or until firm to the touch.
5. Caramel Cream: In a saucepan over medium heat, combine the evaporated milk, condensed milk and butter; bring to a boil. Cook, stirring often, for 10 to 15 minutes, until the sauce thickens and turns a lovely caramel color. Let the pudding cool before unmolding. Serve the warm pudding with a ladle of the warm caramel sauce over top.

SERVES 8

Saskatoon Berry Flan

This recipe appears courtesy of Vincent Parkinson, executive chef at the Calgary Golf and Country Club — and captain of culinary Team Alberta (Team Canada) for the 1996 Culinary Olympics in Berlin and the 1997 World Culinary Cup.

PREHEAT OVEN TO 350° F (180° C)

1 cup	butter	250 mL
1 cup	granulated sugar	250 mL
4	eggs	4
1 cup	all-purpose flour	250 mL
1 cup	ground almonds	250 mL
8 oz	Saskatoon berries *or* blueberries	250 g
1/4 cup	apple jelly	50 mL

1. In a mixing bowl with an electric mixer, cream butter and sugar. Gradually beat in the eggs. Lightly mix in the flour and ground almonds. Spread the batter in a greased pie pan or springform pan.

2. Sprinkle the berries over the dough and bake in preheated oven for 30 minutes.

3. Chill flan. In a saucepan over medium heat, melt apple jelly. Spread over top of flan evenly to glaze. Cool before cutting into wedges to serve.

SERVES 8

Rhubarb and Strawberry Crumb Pie

Here's the perfect dessert for May and June, when fresh straw-berries and young rhubarb appear in the prairie garden. This recipe was shared by my newspaper colleague, Debra Cummings.

PREHEAT OVEN TO 450° F (230° C)

PASTRY FOR A SINGLE CRUST PIE
   (SEE WALNUT PIE, PAGE 176, FOR RECIPE)

3 cups	chopped rhubarb	750 mL
2 cups	sliced fresh strawberries	500 mL
1 1/2 cups	granulated sugar	375 mL
1/3 cup	all-purpose flour	75 mL
1 cup	sour cream	250 mL

Topping
1/2 cup	all-purpose flour	125 mL
1/2 cup	brown sugar	125 mL
1/4 cup	butter, softened	50 mL

1. Arrange rhubarb and strawberries in a 9-inch (23 cm) unbaked pie shell.

2. In a mixing bowl, stir together sugar and 1/3 cup (75 mL) flour with sour cream and pour evenly over fruit.

3. Topping: In a mixing bowl, stir together flour and brown sugar. Cut butter into the flour mixture until crumbly and sprinkle over pie.

4. Bake in preheated oven for 15 minutes. Reduce heat to 375° F (190° C) and bake another 45 minutes, or until fruit is tender. Serve chilled.

Saskatoon Berry Cobbler

*lso called serviceber-
ries, saskatoons grow
wild all over the west-
ern prairies and are
cultivated by some
Alberta farmers. Pick
them in the wild or on
U-pick farms. You can
also look for them at
early July markets (or
substitute blueberries if
you must). Another sug-
gestion: bake this
unique fruit into a
tasty double crust pie.*

PREHEAT OVEN TO 425° F (220° C)
SHALLOW 8-CUP (2 L) OVAL CASSEROLE DISH, GREASED

6 cups	Saskatoon berries	1.5 L
1/2 cup	sugar	125 mL
2 to 3 tbsp	flour	25 to 45 mL

Topping

2 cups	all-purpose flour	500 mL
Pinch	salt	Pinch
3 tbsp	granulated sugar	45 mL
1 tbsp	baking powder	15 mL
1/3 cup	shortening	75 mL
3 tbsp	butter	45 mL
1	egg	1
1/3 cup	milk	75 mL

1. In a bowl combine berries, 1/2 cup (125 mL) sugar and flour; place in casserole dish.

2. In another bowl, combine flour, salt, baking powder and 1 tbsp (15 mL) sugar; work in shortening and butter with a pastry blender, forming coarse crumbs. Lightly beat egg with milk and add to dough, stirring, then kneading lightly to form a smooth (not sticky) pastry.

3. Break off little chunks of the dough, pressing to flatten and placing over filling to form a cobblestone effect, covering entire dish. Sprinkle top with 2 tbsp (25 mL) of sugar and bake in preheated oven for 35 to 45 minutes, until browned and bubbly and dough is cooked through in the center.

SERVES 10

Walnut Pie
with Dried Berries

This rich pie is like a butter tart, with the sweetness offset by the concentrated fruit flavor of dried berries. Serve it in very small slices topped with whipped cream or a dollop of mascarpone triple-cream cheese and a spoonful of tangy fruit compote for balance.

PREHEAT OVEN TO 350° F (180° C)
10-INCH (25 CM) TART PAN *OR* SPRINGFORM PAN

Crust

1 1/4 cups	all-purpose flour	300 mL
1 tbsp	granulated sugar	15 mL
Pinch	salt	Pinch
1/2 cup	butter *or* margarine, cold	125 mL
1	egg yolk	1
1 tbsp	milk	15 mL

Filling

2 cups	walnut pieces	500 mL
4	eggs	4
1/2 cup	granulated sugar	125 mL
1 cup	corn syrup	250 mL
1/2 cup	melted butter	125 mL
1 tbsp	all-purpose flour	15 mL
2 tbsp	Grand Marnier *or* frozen orange juice concentrate	25 mL
	Grated zest of 2 oranges	
1 tsp	vanilla	5 mL
Pinch	salt	Pinch
1 1/2 cups	dried cranberries and/or blueberries (you can also substitute raisins or currants for a sweeter pie)	375 mL

Fruit Compote

4	oranges	4
1 cup	fresh or frozen cranberries *or* blueberries	250 mL
1/2 cup	granulated sugar	125 mL
1/2 cup	orange juice	125 mL
1 tbsp	orange juice *or* Grand Marnier	15 mL

1. Pie shell: Place flour, sugar, salt and butter in food processor; process until crumbly. Add the egg yolk and milk; pulse until dough forms a ball. Wrap dough in plastic and chill 1 hour or overnight. (Pastry can be made in a mixing bowl using pastry cutter if food processor is unavailable.)

2. Roll out dough and use to line tart pan or springform pan. Press to fill in any cracks. Line with foil weighted with 2 cups (500 mL) rice or beans; bake in preheated oven for 20 minutes. Gently remove foil and rice or beans and bake 10 minutes longer.

3. Filling: Toast walnuts in the oven on a baking sheet for 5 minutes; cool. In a mixing bowl, whisk together eggs, sugar, syrup, butter, Grand Marnier, zest, vanilla and salt. Stir in cooled nuts and dried berries. Pour filling into pie shell. Set on a baking sheet in the oven. Bake for 35 to 40 minutes or until filling is set.

4. Compote: Using a sharp knife, cut all the skin and pith from oranges. Working over a bowl to catch any juices, cut flesh from membranes. Cook cranberries and sugar with orange juice, stirring over low heat until berries soften and just begin to pop (about 5 minutes). Remove from heat and stir in orange sections and orange juice (or Grand Marnier). Serve slices of pie with chilled compote on the side.

MAKES 3 TRADITIONAL GRADUATED CAKES

Mom's Dark Christmas Cake with Currants

While some people love them and others hate them, fruit cakes are always part of the Christmas dessert table at many prairie family homes. This dark fruit cake is also used traditionally for wedding cakes and other celebrations. Make it any time and take it skiing or backpacking for instant fuel. This is my Mom, Norah Chavich's recipe — truly one of the tastiest dark fruit cakes you'll find.

4 cups	raisins	1 L
4 cups	currants	1 L
4 cups	red candied cherries	1 L
4 cups	green candied cherries	1 L
4 cups	dates	1 L
2 1/2 cups	chopped walnuts	625 mL
2 1/2 cups	blanched, slivered almonds	625 mL
1 1/4 cups	chopped pecans	300 mL
1 cup	glazed fruit or candied peel	250 mL
1/2 cup	rum, scotch or other liqueur for soaking (optional)	125 mL

Batter

2 cups	butter	500 mL
2 cups	granulated sugar	500 mL
12	eggs	12
3/4 cup	orange juice	175 mL
1/4 cup	molasses	50 mL
4 cups	all-purpose flour	1 L
2 tbsp	allspice	25 mL
2 tbsp	cinnamon	25 mL
2 tbsp	nutmeg	25 mL

1. Wash raisins and currants the night before you plan to bake. Cut cherries in half and chop dates and walnuts. Combine fruit with a little rum, scotch or liqueur (like Irish Mist), if you like, and let soak overnight.

2. In a bowl with an electric mixer, cream together butter and sugar; increase speed and beat until fluffy. Beat in eggs, one at a time.

3. In a separate bowl, stir together flour, allspice, cinnamon and nutmeg. In another bowl, mix orange juice and molasses. Add alternately to creamed mixture until combined.

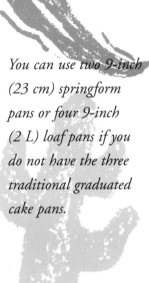

You can use two 9-inch (23 cm) springform pans or four 9-inch (2 L) loaf pans if you do not have the three traditional graduated cake pans.

4. Drain fruit, reserving liqueur. Fold fruit into batter with nuts.

5. Pour batter into 3 greased, graduated cake pans lined with parchment paper and bake at 275° F (140° C) for 2 1/2 to 3 1/2 hours, until a tester in the center of the cake comes out clean. Baking times vary as, traditionally, cake pan sizes vary. Place a bowl of water in oven while baking to keep cakes moist.

6. Cool in pans, remove and brush with reserved liqueur if using. Wrapped tightly in foil, these cakes keep frozen or refrigerated indefinitely. Makes 3 graduated cakes: one each of 8 oz (250 g), 1 lb (500 g) and 2 lbs (1kg).

MAKES 1 CAKE OR 8 TO 10 SLICES

EP Ranch Christmas Cake

The EP Ranch south of Calgary certainly has one of the most colorful histories of the Alberta ranches. Started in 1884 on Pekisko Creek, the ranch caught the eye of crown prince Edward during a visit in 1919. The Prince of Wales purchased the 4,000-acre ranch and renamed it EP (for Edward Prince). He owned the EP for 43 years, visiting three times during the 1920s, sometimes traveling incognito as "Lord Renfrew."

Edward became king in 1936, but abdicated a year later to marry Wallace Simpson. While Edward loved cowboys and ranch life, the new Duchess of Windsor preferred a suite at the Palliser Hotel.

This recipe comes from Buzzards Cowboy Cuisine in Calgary.

1 cup	chopped dates	250 mL
1 cup	boiling water	250 mL
1 tsp	baking soda	5 mL
1/4 cup	butter	50 mL
1 cup	granulated sugar	250 mL
1	egg	1
1 tsp	vanilla	5 mL
1 1/2 cups	all-purpose flour	375 mL
1 tsp	baking powder	5 mL
Pinch	salt	Pinch

Icing

1/2 cup	brown sugar	125 mL
1/3 cup	butter	75 mL
1/2 cup	flaked coconut	125 mL
3 tbsp	half-and-half cream *or* milk	45 mL
1/2 cup	chopped walnuts	125 mL

1. In a saucepan over medium-high heat, combine dates and boiling water. Reduce heat and simmer until dates are soft, about 5 minutes. Add baking soda to dates and keep on the heat for 10 seconds until mixture becomes puffy.
2. In a bowl cream butter and sugar until fluffy; add egg and vanilla. In a separate bowl, combine flour and baking powder with salt and add to batter, mixing well.
3. Add dates to batter and mix well.
4. Pour into a 9-inch (2 L) springform pan that has been greased and floured. Bake at 350° F (180° C) for 60 minutes or until firm to the touch. Cool on a wire rack for 10 minutes, then remove from pan.
5. Icing: In a medium saucepan, heat sugar and butter over medium heat, with coconut and cream. When heated through, stir in walnuts. Remove from heat and spread over cooled cake, allowing the icing to drizzle down the sides of the cake. Place under the broiler for about 45 seconds, until the mixture starts to bubble.
6. Serve sliced, warm or cold, with whipped cream.

Chocolate Diablo Cake

The recipe for this devilish layer cake comes from Marianne Sanders, one of Calgary's best-loved pastry chefs. Marianne adds cinnamon, chili peppers and peppercorns to the mousse that forms both the batter and the filling for this intriguing chocolate cake. You can barely taste the hot stuff, but it enhances the dark chocolate flavor and makes this a cake to challenge the taste buds. Cut into 2 triangular layers, it also makes for a gorgeous presentation, surrounded by fresh fruit.

*Safety tips for using raw eggs: Buy eggs from a reputable source; make sure they have been refrigerated and are kept that way; use within date on box; finally, **never use eggs that are cracked!***

PREHEAT OVEN TO 350° F (180° C)
**JELLY ROLL PAN, ABOUT 7 1/2 x 11 x 3/4 INCHES
(45 x 29 x 2 CM), LINED WITH PARCHMENT PAPER**

1 cup+ 2 tbsp	butter	250 mL + 25 mL
1 cup	granulated sugar	250 mL
1 tsp	cinnamon	5 mL
1 tsp	dried chilies and mixed peppercorns, ground together in equal proportions	5 mL
10	eggs, separated	10
10 oz	Callebaut semisweet chocolate or other good Belgian chocolate	300g

Glaze

8 oz	Callebaut semisweet chocolate	250 g
1 cup	whipping (35%) cream	250 mL

1. Cake: In a bowl using an electric mixer, beat butter and 3/4 cup (175 mL) of the sugar together until fluffy. Add the spices. Beat in egg yolks one at a time.

2. Melt chocolate in a double boiler or a bowl over saucepan of simmering water; cool slightly and stir into the batter. Using clean beaters, beat the egg whites with remaining sugar until stiff and fold into the batter. Set aside 1 1/2 cups (375 mL) batter in refrigerator. Spread remaining batter in lined jelly roll pan. Bake in preheated oven for 30 minutes. Allow cake to cool. (It will fall a certain amount.)

3. Cut the cake into 4 equal rectangles; assemble into a rectangular layer cake spread with remaining batter between layers. (Do this on a board or plate; the cake will be hard to move later.) Cut cake on the diagonal, forming 2 triangular cakes for presentation. Refrigerate until chilled and set.

4. In a double boiler (or bowl placed over a saucepan of simmering water), melt chocolate and whipping cream together to form the glaze.

5. Set chilled cakes on a rack over a pan to catch drips and pour glaze over, smoothing the top and drizzling over the sides to coat with a wide spatula, carefully transfer cakes to a serving platter. Serve cakes garnished with fresh fruit.

Oatmeal Chocolate Chippers

These big, grainy cookies are filled with chunks of three kinds of chocolate. I use the great chocolate offered by Calgary's own Belgium chocolatier, Bernard Callebaut. Any good chocolate will do, but the better the chocolate, the better the cookie.

For this (and all) my cookie recipes, I use a double-layer insulated cookie sheet which I love. It makes perfect cookies that never burn on the bottom.

PREHEAT OVEN TO 375° F (190° C)
BAKING SHEET, GREASED

1 3/4 cups	rolled oats	425 mL
1/2 cup	butter at room temperature	125 mL
1/2 cup	granulated sugar	125 mL
1/2 cup	packed light brown sugar	125 mL
1	egg	1
1 tsp	vanilla	5 mL
1 cup	all-purpose flour	250 mL
1/2 tsp	baking powder	2 mL
1/2 tsp	baking soda	2 mL
1/4 tsp	salt	1 mL
1/2 cup	chopped milk chocolate	125 mL
1/2 cup	chopped white chocolate	125 mL
1/2 cup	chopped almonds	125 mL
1/3 cup	semisweet chocolate chips	75 mL

1. Place 1 1/2 cups (375 mL) oats in the container of a food processor and process for 1 minute or until you have a fine oat flour.

2. In a mixing bowl, beat the butter with both the sugars until fluffy and beat in the egg and the vanilla.

3. In a separate bowl, combine the processed oats with the flour, baking powder, baking soda and salt. Slowly add to the butter mixture. Then fold in the remaining 1/4 cup (50 mL) of oats, the chopped milk and white chocolates, chopped almonds and chocolate chips.

4. Spoon about 1 tbsp (15 mL) batter onto cookie sheet and bake in preheated oven until golden, about 10 minutes. Cool slightly on the sheets before removing the cookies. They will be soft but will get crunchier as they cool.

MAKES 3 DOZEN COOKIES

Oatmeal Peanut Butter Cookies

Here's another way to use Alberta oats in a big, healthy cookie.

PREHEAT OVEN TO 350° F (180° C)
BAKING SHEETS, GREASED

1 1/2 cups	rolled oats	375 mL
1 cup	whole wheat flour	250 mL
1/2 tsp	baking powder	2 mL
1/2 tsp	baking soda	2 mL
1/2 tsp	salt	2 mL
1/2 cup	butter, softened	125 mL
1/3 cup	crunchy peanut butter	75 mL
1 cup	brown sugar	250 mL
1/2 cup	granulated sugar	125 mL
1	egg	1
2 tbsp	water	25 mL
1/2 tsp	vanilla	2 mL

1. In a bowl combine oats, flour, baking powder, baking soda and salt.

2. In another bowl, cream butter with peanut butter, brown sugar and granulated sugar. Beat in egg, water and vanilla.

3. Gradually add dry ingredients to creamed mixture, stirring until well-mixed. Spoon by rounded tbsp (15 mL) onto baking sheets about 2 inches (5 cm) apart and bake in preheated oven for 12 to 15 minutes or until golden.

MAKES 2 DOZEN COOKIES

Nutricookies

These big cookies, chock-full of grains and seeds, make a filling breakfast on the run. The recipe comes from the Heartland Country Store in Calgary. They're great with a cappuccino for breakfast, or taken on the hiking trail for a high-energy snack.

Most cattle drives were dry affairs and cowboys consumed an awful lot of campfire coffee — some say a crew would consume a pound a day. To make good campfire coffee, you need an old granite-ware pot, coarsely ground coffee and cold water.

Johnny Chinook said "coffee should be strong enough to float a two-bit piece." That's the way real cowboys like it.

PREHEAT OVEN TO 350° F (180° C)
BAKING SHEETS, GREASED

2 cups	butter, at room temperature	500 mL
2 cups	brown sugar	500 mL
4	eggs	4
1/4 cup	buttermilk	50 mL
2 cups	whole wheat flour	500 mL
2 cups	unbleached flour	500 mL
4 cups	rolled oats (large flake oats)	1 L
1/4 cup	bran	50 mL
2 tsp	baking soda	10 mL
1 tbsp	baking powder	15 mL
1 1/2 cups	chocolate chips	375 mL
1/2 cup	slivered almonds	125 mL
1/4 cup	raw sunflower seeds	50 mL

1. In a bowl cream butter and sugar. Beat in eggs, one at a time; mix in buttermilk.

2. In a separate bowl, combine whole wheat flour, unbleached flour, oats, bran, baking soda, baking powder, chocolate chips, almonds and sunflower seeds until mixed. Stir into creamed mixture until well blended.

3. Scoop about 1/2 cup (125 mL) dough onto baking sheet, flattening into a cookie shape (these cookies don't spread much). Bake for 15 to 20 minutes or until golden brown.

Cowboy Coffee

1. Fill pot to just below spout. Add 1 tablespoon (15 mL) coffee for every 1 cup (250 mL) water, plus one more for the pot. Set over the fire, bring to a boil until it starts to simmer and steam. Remove from fire; add 1 cup (250 mL) cold water to settle grounds on bottom of pot. Serve.

Index